The Theology of the Hammer

Millard Fuller has worked on construction at many Habitat building sites around the world. Here, with hammer in hand, he works away at the 1991 Jimmy Carter Work Project in Miami, Florida.

The Theology of the Hammer

by **Millard Fuller**
President and Founder
Habitat for Humanity

Smyth & Helwys Publishing, Inc.
Macon, Georgia

ISBN1-880837-92-7

The Theology of the Hammer
by Millard Fuller

Printed in the United Sates of America. The paper used in this publication meets the minimum requirements of American National Standard for Information Sciences—Permanence of Paper for Printed Library Materials, ANSI Z39.48-1984.

Unless otherwise noted, all scripture quotations are from The Holy Bible, New International Version Copyright © 1973, 1978, 1984 by International Bible Society. Used by permission of Zondervan Bible Publishers.

"The Excitement Is Building" by Norton M. Wade, Copyright © 1990 NORTUNES, is used by permission.

All proceeds from the royalties on this book will be used to help eliminate poverty housing all over the world.

Library of Congress Cataloging-in-Publication Data

Fuller, Millard, 1935–
    The theology of the hammer / Millard Fuller.
    vi + 154pp.   6 x 9" (15 x 23 cm.)
    ISBN 1-880837-92-7
    1. Habitat for Humanity, Inc. 2. Habitat for Humanity International, Inc. 3. Church work with the poor—Societies, etc.
4. Housing—Religious aspects—Christianity—Societies, etc.
5. Poor—Housing—Societies, etc. I. Title.
BV4407.63.F85 1994
261.8'325—dc20   94-4737
                                     CIP

Contents

To my precious wife, Linda,
my best friend, partner, and sweetheart for life.

Introduction

Getting Started

In a sense, I have been writing *The Theology of the Hammer* since 1965. In 1992, the book moved a step closer to reality when the Habitat for Humanity International board of directors asked me to expand to book length a chapter by the same title in my 1986 book, *No More Shacks!*

I was excited about the project, but I had many other things to do. As president of Habitat for Humanity International, I have numerous responsibilities and tasks to perform, including extensive correspondence and scores of speaking engagements all over the United States, across Canada and in many other countries.

In the midst of all this, I made preparations to start work on the new book. I wrote Clyde Tilley, a former Habitat for Humanity International Board member who has published numerous articles and some books on theology, asking for his ideas about the proposed book. In addition, I sent a memorandum to every location around the world where Habitat for Humanity is at work, asking for stories or examples of "the theology of the hammer."

Many recipients of my memorandum responded with scores of stories and other ideas.

Rick Beech, then directing our Habitat program in the South Central region of the United States, wrote me that his assistant, Pam Campbell, was a talented writer who was interested in helping with this project. I quickly agreed to her involvement and assigned her to do research on the ecumenical movement, which encourages different churches and church organizations to work together. Chapter seven, "A Theology of Unity," is largely Pam's work; she also helped in many other ways, including extensive editing.

My wife, Linda, frequently travels with me now that our four children are grown. Because of our heavy schedules, I was unable to set aside time on my calendar to begin putting my thoughts for the book on paper until November 1992. Shortly before my target date for writing, Linda said from an adjacent airplane seat, "I can't go away with you to start working on your book. I've got to stay home for a while." (She is essential to the writing process, transferring my handwritten drafts to a word processor for editing and giving valuable advice on the style and content of every chapter.)

I understood her feelings because I, too, was really drained. I had already realized that, perhaps, we were pushing too hard and traveling

too much when I got up one night on one of our trips to go to the bathroom and walked into a wall. The bathroom was there the night before!
Anyway, we just canceled the time set aside for book writing in November and got reacquainted with our house and offices in Americus.

After a few days at home, we were re-energized and ready to write.
Bob and Pat Dean, good friends and Habitat partners from Marietta,
Georgia, had kindly allowed us to use their beautiful "Seabreeze" cabin
at Grayton Beach, near Destin, Florida, as a place for rest and renewal.
There, in early December 1992, Linda and I retreated so that I could begin
the long-delayed project of writing *The Theology of the Hammer.*

The Bible is my primary resource for everything I write. The foundation stone on which both this book and the work of Habitat for Humanity
are built, it is my constant companion. I carry my personal Bible, a rather
large one, in my briefcase on all my trips. Often, the person who meets
me at an airport will grab my briefcase and exclaim how heavy it is. I
always respond that it is heavy because the Word of God is in it, and that
Word is heavy!

Among other resources I used, in addition to my Bible and the contri-
butions of Habitat folks, were *A Theology for the Social Gospel* by Walter
Rauchenbusch; *Out of My Life and Thought* by Albert Schweitzer; *Thomas
Merton: Spiritual Master, The Essential Writings; How Much Is Enough?* by
Alan Durning; *In the Name of Jesus* by Henri J. M. Nouwen; and *Loaves and
Fishes* by Dorothy Day. All of these materials, to one extent or another,
have influenced and helped me in the writing of this book.

The person, though, who influenced and inspired me the most was
Clarence Jordan, the humble scholar with a doctoral degree in Greek New
Testament from the Southern Baptist Theological Seminary who became
so well known for his "Cotton Patch" translations of the New Testament,
and who was the principal founder and leader of the Christian community of Koinonia Farm near Americus, Georgia.

I first met Clarence in December 1965, when Linda and I went to
Koinonia at a time of great personal crisis in our lives. We had decided
to leave a life of affluence and success in business in Montgomery,
Alabama, in order to find new life in Christian service.

I have always felt that God led us to Clarence Jordan at that particular
time, just a few years before his death on October 29, 1969. He was a man
full of grace, kindness, and the love of Jesus. I had never met anyone
before, and I have not met anyone since, who was so completely in touch
and in tune with Jesus. To me, he actually thought like Jesus! He was a
practical man who loved God, his fellow man, and the land, which he
considered a sacred gift from God.

When Linda and I first went to Koinonia we intended to spend only
a couple of hours but ended up staying a month and then returning twice

for a total of nearly six years. We were captivated by Koinonia and especially by Clarence!

During that initial month, Clarence and I talked a lot about theology and practical Christian discipleship. It was the peak of the shipping season for the pecans and pecan products, the sales of which, at that time, the small community largely supported itself. The desire of those who joined Clarence and his wife, Florence, was to live in Christian community, much as the early Christians had done as described in Acts 2 and 4. At first—the community was started in 1942—they had sustained themselves by raising chickens and other farm animals, along with various crops. The farm produce was sold to customers in Americus and to people in other towns in the county as well as at a roadside market along nearby U.S. Highway 19, then the principal route of tourists traveling to and from Florida.

In the late 1950s, when feelings about integration were so intense in the South, the local White Citizens Council and the Ku Klux Klan turned on Koinonia with a vengeance because the farm was racially integrated. Clarence felt strongly that "in Christ, there is neither Greek nor Jew, slave nor free, male nor female; for you are all one in Christ Jesus" (Gal 3:28). In a south Georgia setting, he believed that statement meant there should be no distinction between white and black and certainly no discrimination against anybody! The Koinonia community was also suspect because of its total commitment to non-violence and economic sharing.

First, the roadside market was burned. As soon as it was rebuilt, the market was bombed and totally destroyed. Nightriders began to shoot into Koinonia houses. Another building was burned. When Koinonia people went into Americus, they were harassed and sometimes physically attacked. Then, a total boycott was imposed against the farm in a concerted attempt to force the community out. At that point, Clarence and his fellow community members started the pecan-shelling and fruitcake- and candy-making business as a way to survive. Clarence, always with a sense of humor in the face of even the worst adversity, coined the mail-order advertising slogan, "Help us ship the nuts out of Georgia!"

I helped him do just that. Very often, between packing shipments of the various pecan products, we would stop, put our feet up on the packing table, and get into lengthy discussions about God, racism, greed, discipleship to Christ in our day and age, the meaning of life, how to be an authentic peacemaker, and much more. Talking with Clarence Jordan was absolutely a joy—beyond words to describe! I sought every opportunity to be with him and to have more in-depth discussions with him.

At that time, the farm had a cow that Clarence milked the old fashioned way—by hand. I, too, knew how to milk, having often done so as a boy back in the outskirts of Lanett, Alabama, where I grew up. I lost no time in signing up as his "assistant milker." Each morning and again in the evening, we would go to the barn. Clarence would sit on one side of the cow and milk two teats and I, on the other side, would take care of the other two. As we squirted milk into the bucket, we each leaned our heads toward the back of the cow and talked theology between her tail and hind legs.

People often ask me if I have attended seminary. I always reply, "Yes, I packed pecans and milked an old cow with Clarence Jordan; and as we did these tasks together, he taught me about obedience to Christ and authentic participation in God's work in the world. Yes, I believe I've been to seminary!"

Clarence introduced me to "the God movement" (his term for the kingdom of God), to the concept of being God's partner and partners with one another to do God's work in the world. He also introduced me to the clear imperative in the Gospels to act out our faith. Clarence often exclaimed that people would "worship the hind legs off of Jesus but they wouldn't obey him." He said that much of modern-day religious practice was irrelevant, concerned with mere ritual and the reading and telling of ancient Bible stories, with little or no application in today's world.

In an attempt to change such ways of "being religious," Clarence translated most of the New Testament into his "Cotton Patch" version in which he placed Jesus in Georgia and substituted whites and blacks for Jews and Samaritans. He said that we in south Georgia had little trouble between Jews and Samaritans, but we did have a black-white problem. The issue, he said, was relevant religion. Jesus, he pointed out, was relevant in his day and we, as the continuing body of Christ, should also be relevant and radically faithful to Christ.

Putting faith into practice and being relevant is at the very heart of "the theology of the hammer." Therefore, a few years later, Linda and I returned to Koinonia to work with Clarence and others to launch a new ministry called "Koinonia Partners" that included a component of building houses for needy families. (After our month at Koinonia, Linda and I left to pursue other interests. We came back in mid-1968.)

Substandard housing was a real problem in the area and nobody was doing anything about it. The first program, called "partnership housing," was the forerunner of Habitat for Humanity, which was formed in 1976 (after Linda and I, along with our children, had spent three years building houses in Zaire, Central Africa). But I am getting ahead of myself.

Here, I simply want to acknowledge the wonderful contributions of all who helped make this book possible. In addition to those persons already named, our dear friend Doralee Robertson of Jacksonville, Florida—who helped so much with the editing of our 1990 book, *The Excitement Is Building* (Word, 1990)—did extensive editing work; and Jim Purks, senior writer at Habitat's international headquarters, spent countless hours helping with the editing, researching, and verifying of much material in virtually all of the chapters. Jim was the key person in coordinating all the work on the manuscript, including the appendixes and photographs and then working with the publisher. I express profound gratitude to Jim for his extraordinary contribution to this book.

I also want to express appreciation to Habitat staffer Paul Pegler, who assisted with research and verification. Many thanks go to Doug Bright, head of Habitat for Humanity International's communication services department, who, with his dedicated staff, helped in various ways. A genuine word of thanks, too, goes to Cecil P. Staton, Jr., publisher of Smyth and Helwys, and his staff for working so harmoniously with us to get this book published.

Finally, I owe a word of gratitude to Chrys and John Street of Marietta, Georgia, who graciously allowed Linda and me to use their beautiful "Glencove" on Lake Rabun in north Georgia for much of the writing of this book, and to Kirby and Joan Godsey of Macon, Georgia, who allowed us to use their condominium at St. Simons Island on the east coast of Georgia for still more writing. To all of these people I extend heartfelt thanks. Without their good help this book would not have been possible. I acknowledge and express appreciation for each one.

I hope what follows is meaningful to you.

Linda Fuller, co-founder of Habitat for Humanity, skillfully handles a paint brush as work nears completion on the first house in Americus to be sponsored, funded, and built completely by women who organized WATCH—Women Accepting the Challenge of Housing. (Photo by Julie Lopez)

Joined by Linda Fuller (front row left) members of Girl Scout Troop 227 proudly gather in front of the house they built in partnership with Habitat for Humanity of Greater Greensboro, North Carolina.

Chapter 1

A New Concept

I cannot recall the first time I used the phrase, "the theology of the hammer." I gave a lecture with that same title at Chautauqua Institute in western New York in 1987. I had been using the term long before that, though.

What does "the theology of the hammer" mean? Succeeding chapters seek to answer that question more fully, but, simply stated, the idea or concept of "the theology of the hammer" is that our Christian faith (indeed, our entire Judeo-Christian tradition) mandates that we do more than just talk about faith and sing about love. We must put faith and love into action to make them real, to make them come alive for people. Faith must be incarnated; that is to say, it must become more than a verbal proclamation or an intellectual assent. True faith must be acted out.

Within the context of Habitat for Humanity, "the theology of the hammer" dictates that the nail be hit on the head—literally, and repeatedly —until the house is built and the needy family moves in. It means, too, that continuing love and concern must be shown to the family to ensure success as a new homeowner.

This theology is also about bringing a wide diversity of people, churches, and other organizations together to build houses and establish viable and dynamic communities. It is acknowledging that differences of opinion exist on numerous subjects—political, philosophical, and theological—but that we can find common ground in using a hammer as an instrument to manifest God's love. Even though there may be strong differences on all sorts of things—baptism, communion, what night to have prayer meeting, and how the preacher should dress, for example—we can agree on the imperative of the gospel to serve others in the name of the Lord.

We can agree on building and renovating simple, decent houses with and for God's people in need and in doing so using biblical economics: no profit and no interest; taking what limited resources are available, asking God to bless them, then going to work, and proceeding with the sure knowledge that God's love extends to everyone—with a preferential concern for the poor.[1]

Another important aspect of "the theology of the hammer" is the belief that we are called by God to the work of housing the world's poor. Our goal in Habitat for Humanity is to completely eliminate poverty housing and homelessness. We will accomplish that lofty goal by making shelter a matter of conscience. Our intention is to make substandard housing and homelessness socially, politically, morally, and religiously unacceptable. We believe we can accomplish what we have set out to do because God has called us, because we are seeking to follow God's leading in the work, and because the Bible assures us that, with God, all things are possible.

This will all be done by starting more and more Habitat projects throughout the United States, Canada, Mexico, and around the world. As of early 1994, there were over 1,000 Habitat affiliates in towns and cities in all fifty states of the United States and the District of Columbia, and another 163 Habitat organizations in forty other countries building houses in more than 600 cities, towns, and villages. These groups, supported financially and helped personally by hundreds of thousands of individuals and churches and other organizations, are building thousands of houses each year. Before the end of the decade, we should be building more than 40,000 houses a year.

We want to continue, dramatically and rapidly, to expand the work of Habitat for Humanity. As soon as possible, we want to build Habitat houses in every town, county, and parish in the United States; in every province in Canada; and in every nation on the earth. The Bible teaches that God is the God of the whole crowd. Ninety-nine sheep in the corral are not acceptable. Only the entire flock of 100 is pleasing to God. As long as any person or any family is outside, our mandate is to invite them in. Why? Because, as Christ said, "Whatever you did for one of the least of these brothers of mine, you did for me" (Matt 25:40).

Dick Fernstrum, a long-time and dedicated Habitat partner, experienced a very humbling moment in regard to "one of the least." He shared that experience in a speech at a dedication service for six Habitat houses in Tucson, Arizona:

> My first exposure to Habitat for Humanity was when a group of eleven of us from First Presbyterian Church of Sarasota, Florida, went to Immokalee, Florida, to spend a week working on a Habitat house. Immokalee is a farming community of 10,000 people in south Florida, the majority of whom are migrant farm worker families.
>
> The house we were to work on was the last in a row of six on a new street. The block walls were up, the trusses were set, and the plywood was on the trusses.
>
> The newest Habitat family on the block was the Perez family, right next door. They had a bunch of little kids—there must have been five or six of them.
>
> Each morning as we began to work, out came the Perez children, freshly scrubbed and neatly dressed. They were constantly under foot and always eager to help.

As far as I was concerned, the presence of the children was unsafe, annoying and an interference we didn't need. It didn't occur to me that by their willing presence they were trying to express gratitude for their home—a home that had been made possible by the numerous donors and volunteers who were strangers to these kids. To me, the kids were just in the way!

On our last day, we finished the roof. I was one of four people nailing shingles. I put down my hammer to get another package of shingles. When I returned, I found this little boy up on the roof. I told him to move away, to go back down; he was interfering with my work. But he didn't, so I told him again—rather rudely, I suppose.

A co-worker said, "He only wants to help you, Dick. Why don't you let him hand you the nails?" So I did—but still not very cheerfully. I told him that if he could do it right and he obeyed me, he could help. I showed him where to squat and how to get the nails out of my nail apron and hand them to me one at a time as I placed the shingles. I was still being quite crabby, but he was very agreeable.

As we began, I said to him, "If you're going to be my partner, I'll have to know who you are. My name is Dick. What is yours?" He looked up at me with his round dark eyes and a big smile and said, "I am Jesus."

Well, you remember that Paul was struck blind on the road to Damascus. This wasn't quite as awesome for me. But it sure had an impact, and continues to challenge me to this day.

In addition to building Habitat houses in more and more places, we want to expand our partnership with other non-profit groups, to help them and to enhance their work (and have ours enhanced!)—even if not officially associated with Habitat for Humanity. Some of the organizations we have already been working with are World Vision, Prison Fellowship, The Enterprise Foundation, and Heifer Project International. We also pursue partnerships with companies, associations, and other organizations to help accomplish our goal of getting everybody in the world into a decent place to live. This, too, is a vital part of "the theology of the hammer."

We seek to focus attention on the issue of shelter in other ways. We write articles and books and publish a newspaper, *Habitat World*, which is read by over one million people every two months. Habitat produces videos and television programs, sponsors conferences, and displays materials at conferences of other organizations. Our speakers bureau sends persons out across the land to tell the Habitat story and encourage people to get involved to eliminate poverty housing and homelessness.

Another important approach for getting the word out is by soliciting churches to support the work in a variety of ways, including becoming "covenant churches" or joining the "Adopt-A-House" program to build houses for poor families. Furthermore, Habitat for Humanity International and local affiliates sponsor marathon walks, bike rides, building blitzes, and many other special events. The entire Habitat organization observes an "International Day of Prayer and Action for Human Habitat" on the third Sunday of September each year.

Special projects like "all women-built houses" dramatize our cause and challenge more people to join us. This initiative was pioneered by Habitat for Humanity of Charlotte, North Carolina.[2]

One of the most exciting ventures ever launched by Habitat for Humanity is the Sumter County Initiative. The genesis of this undertaking was the Habitat Board meeting and retreat in Atlanta in January 1992 where the idea surfaced to write this book on "the theology of the hammer."

Ever since we started building houses for needy families, I have dreamed of completely eliminating poverty housing in our home area of Americus and Sumter County, Georgia. Forever etched in my memory is the experience of moving Bo and Emma Johnson and their children into their new home at Koinonia Farm in 1969. Their house was the first one ever to be built through this ministry. As director of Koinonia at the time, I witnessed family after family move into their new houses over the next few years. The joy of each of them and of all who helped build the houses was an incredible blessing.

After spending three years in Zaire, in Central Africa, building houses for needy families, I returned with my family to south Georgia in late 1976 to found Habitat for Humanity. The following year, just one block south of our little headquarters on West Church Street in Americus, we built our first Habitat house in the town.

We discovered a very poor middle-aged couple just down the street living in a pitiful, unpainted shack with great holes in the floor, a leaky roof, a spigot in the front yard as their only water supply, and no toilet facilities. Fred and Marie Postell were using a big clump of bushes in the back yard as their toilet! Fred had worked for years for a nearby small industry, but he had suffered a mild stroke a few years earlier and could no longer work. Marie was quite thin and seemed perpetually tired.

I found out who owned the property and was able to persuade the owner to sell to us. We promptly started building a new house for the Postells in front of the old shack. As you can imagine, Fred and Marie were thrilled. The work went quickly and soon the house was finished. It was modest with two bedrooms, a living room, a kitchen-dining room combination, and a bathroom. To Fred and Marie, the house was like a palace. As we were bringing their meager belongings from their shack into the new house, Marie exclaimed, "I wish my mamma had lived to see me today moving into our new house!" She was so happy.

Unfortunately, a week after moving in, Marie became ill. She was taken to the hospital and diagnosed as having inoperable cancer. After a few days in the hospital, she returned home. A month later, she was dead.

Bill Givens, a local pastor who had been involved in the building of the house for the Postells, wrote a moving article for the newspaper entitled "Death in a Decent House." Marie was fifty years old when she died. Her life had been lived in shacks, but she died in dignity—in a clean, new, decent place. She had a month in a really good house.

Since the building of the Postell house, Habitat and Koinonia's "partnership housing" program had steadily constructed houses. By early 1992, nearly 300 homes had been completed in the city and county. Shacks in many slum neighborhoods were completely eradicated and replaced with modest, but good and solid, houses. In the immediate vicinity of our headquarters, Habitat volunteer builders had continued to tear down dilapidated old houses and replace them with new ones. In 1985, one block west of the first office, we started erecting a new headquarters building, which covered an entire city block. To the east and south was a sea of shacks. Within five years, they were all gone and over fifty new houses stood in their place.

Many shacks remained throughout the city and county, however. Although I had not done a careful study, my estimate was that we needed to build or renovate approximately 500 more houses in Americus and Sumter County to completely eliminate substandard housing. At our then-current building rate of about five houses a year in Sumter County, the job would be finished in a hundred years! I wanted to see poverty housing eliminated in our home area in my lifetime, and I did not think I would live that long.

Therefore, I presented a bold proposal to the Habitat International board of directors in January 1992, to launch an initiative to eliminate all poverty housing in Americus and Sumter County *by the end of the decade*. The proposal was received in stunned silence. Then, people began to speak, some with enthusiastic responses, but more with reservations.

"Why have we not heard of this before? This will require a lot of study."

"A project like this will take millions of dollars. Where will you get the money? It's not in the budget."

"Putting all that much money in Americus and Sumter County will take funds from other work."

"Other Habitat affiliates will take offense at putting so much emphasis on one place."

I countered that such a daring initiative would have an energizing effect on the whole ministry. I said it would be like a beacon of light, an example of what could be done in other places. Our goal everywhere, of course, was to eliminate poverty housing and homelessness, but to actually do it in a specific place would be a powerful demonstration plot. It was only appropriate, I went on to say, for Habitat to eliminate substandard housing in our hometown and county as quickly as possible, since we were advocating that be done in every other place!

Finally, I argued, Habitat for Humanity would only be the catalyst to launch the initiative. We would, of course, continue to be the lead player, but many other groups would join in to realize the goal. These other entities would also help provide the money needed to reach the goal. My idea was to form an umbrella organization that would direct the effort, raise money locally, engage city and county government, mobilize other agencies and churches, and be the ongoing force to keep things moving ahead on schedule.

I had a firm conviction that people in our area would rally behind this idea, although there had been a history of suspicion and even hostility toward Koinonia over the years because of the strong witness there in regard to racial integration, peacemaking, and economic sharing. Habitat for Humanity had inherited some of that suspicion and hostility because of our close historic connection with Koinonia; but, I sensed, times were changing. Local people were more accepting. They had seen the transformations we had made in many neighborhoods and liked what they saw.

Habitat for Humanity had increasingly become an integral part of the Americus/Sumter County community. Habitat's employees and volunteers participated in community activities. They attended local churches, enrolled their children in the school system, and had steadily developed deep relationships with local people.

Furthermore, with the creation of the umbrella group, we would take away all excuses from people because they would not have to support Habitat for Humanity or Koinonia if they did not want to. They could work through another fine local group that had been formed (Christian Rebuilders), or they could work through the city or county government, the housing authority, or through a local church or civic club. People would simply be challenged to do something, one way or another, to realize the goal of a city and county with no shacks and no substandard housing of any kind by the year 2000.

Even before presenting the proposal to the board in Atlanta, I had floated the idea with several key leaders in Americus and Sumter County. The first person I talked to was my good friend, Russell Thomas, Jr., who had served as mayor of Americus for ten years (and who was re-elected mayor in late 1993). He strongly encouraged me and pledged his support. I also talked to the mayor at that time, Tom Gailey, and I called or met with leaders of the Chamber of Commerce, county and state government, churches, and other groups. I enlisted the support of former President

Jimmy Carter. I asked all of these people to write letters of support. Not a single person turned me down. Everyone I contacted was enthusiastic.

I took the letters of support to the board meeting. Even so, some board members were not convinced that we should proceed with the proposal. There was a motion to table the matter until the next board meeting in April. I spoke strongly against the motion for two reasons. First, I felt I had momentum going in Americus and Sumter County and I was sure that a delay would greatly dampen and possibly kill the excitement that had built. Next, I had a person in mind to head the new initiative, and I was afraid we would lose him if we could not offer a job immediately.

Ted Swisher, a Princeton alumnus, had moved to Koinonia right after graduation in 1970. Over the years, he had been involved in all aspects of Koinonia's work, but especially the house building ministry. For several years, he was the director at Koinonia. In 1983, Ted joined our staff at Habitat as the first director of our work in the United States. At that time, we were working in twenty-two locations nationwide. Over the next six years, Ted presided over a rapidly growing program of local Habitat affiliates. By the time he left this position in February 1989 to head Habitat's new work in Australia, the affiliates had grown to over 300 towns and cities. Ted also established a nationwide network of regional offices.

He and his wife, Lisa (who had come to Habitat headquarters in 1987 as a volunteer and married Ted a year later), spent three years in Australia, solidly launching the work there and adding a son, Benjamin, to their young family. In December 1991, they returned to the States with an open future before them.

I could not imagine a better person to guide this new venture than Ted Swisher. I had talked to him about the proposal. He had not given me an answer, but I knew a tabling of the matter for three months would almost certainly foreclose the possibility of his even considering the job.

After lengthy discussion in the board meeting, the motion to table was defeated. Then, it was back to considering the main motion. I thought the time had come for extraordinary action. I wanted to make sure the motion passed.

Ever since we started Habitat for Humanity, I have regularly attended the board meetings. Whenever I have felt strongly about an issue, I would stand to express my opinion. Otherwise, I would speak from a sitting position. On this issue, though, I did not think that standing was enough to show how passionately I felt that we should move ahead without delay. So, for the first time ever, I climbed atop the table in front of me and stood at my full height of six feet, four inches. From that vantage point, I reviewed all the reasons why we should vote to proceed with the proposal to create an organization in Americus and Sumter County that would completely eliminate substandard housing by the end of the decade. After my brief but forceful talk, I jumped down, ran around the room to create more excitement, and then I leaped over the table into the center of the group, got on my knees, and pleaded for a favorable vote.

It worked!

The board not only voted to proceed—the vote was unanimous! I was extremely pleased and grateful for the board's confidence in me and, more importantly, in the idea and possibilities of what had been proposed. The board directed me to bring a more complete proposal to the next meeting in April, including a budget for the first year of the initiative. In the meantime, we were authorized to offer the job of director to Ted Swisher. I returned home full of joy and excitement. I was certain my long-held dream would now come true. The time was right.

George Peagler, an outstanding young attorney in Americus, agreed to head the new group. Organizational meetings were held and the name Sumter County Initiative (SCI) agreed upon. After prayerful consideration, Ted Swisher accepted the job as head of SCI and director of the local Habitat for Humanity affiliate. He, Lisa, and Benjamin moved to Americus early in February.

The response of the community was tremendous. Rudy Hayes, editor of our local paper, *The Americus Times-Recorder*, ran numerous articles—some of them front page, headline stories—about the evolving initiative.

On April 2, 1992, a big "kick-off" dinner was held at Georgia Southwestern College to officially launch the Sumter County Initiative. The event was attended by over a hundred of the leaders of the city and county. Enthusiasm was very high. After the meal, people began to rise spontaneously and announce how they would help. A banker said he would offer loans at a favorable rate for those who did not qualify for a Habitat house but did not have adequate income for a conventional loan. A law firm announced that its partners would build a house. The county pledged support. A local African-American pastor rose to say that his church would pledge at least $1,000 a year.

At the end of the evening, J. Frank Myers, a man who had been mayor several years earlier and who had seen a lot of disharmony in our city and county, handed me a note that said, "Congratulations! I wouldn't have believed it if I hadn't seen it!"

A few weeks later, at the First United Methodist Church, we held a special meeting of church leaders in the city and county. Representatives of thirty-seven churches attended. The excitement and support were building.

Something very dramatic, though, was needed to give high visibility to the budding initiative. I proposed that Habitat blitz-build twenty houses during Holy Week (April 5–11, 1993). The project would be called the 20/20,000 Project because the twentieth house would be the 20,000th house built by Habitat for Humanity worldwide.

It had taken us fifteen years to build the first 10,000 Habitat houses. The 10,000th house had been built in April 1991 in Atlanta by volunteers of John Wieland Homes, Inc., which excels in the construction of single family houses and has long supported Habitat's work. They had built the house in fourteen hours!

It took fourteen months to build the next 5,000 houses. The 15,000th house was part of a twenty-one-house blitz in Evansville, Indiana, in June 1992. Linda and I were there to participate in dedicating that special house and the twenty other houses on Saturday, June 20.

The next 5,000 houses would be completed in only ten months; that put the 20,000th house on schedule for April 1993.

Twenty houses in a week to celebrate the milestone of 20,000 houses built in Habitat's worldwide work was exciting to everyone who heard about the idea. So, we began to plan for it.

The first order of business was to find a plot of land for the houses. Russell Thomas solved that problem with a very generous gift of eighteen beautiful acres on the north edge of the city. It was perfectly located for our needs.

Ted and others enlisted people to put in the streets, utilities, and foundations. The land was large enough for forty houses. We would build the twenty in April and the remaining twenty later.

Clive Rainey, a very faithful and effective Habitat staff member in our development department, started lining up sponsors for the houses. He was a natural for the task because he had been with Habitat almost from the beginning and knew just about everyone in town.

The cost would be an average of $20,000 for each house. Citizens Bank of Americus quickly agreed to build the twentieth house. First United Methodist Church committed to build a house. First Presbyterian and Bethesda Baptist formed a partnership to build a house together, as did Allen Chapel African Methodist Episcopal and Calvary Episcopal. Koinonia made a commitment to supervise the building of the "Tom Hall house." Tom, a greatly beloved Habitat staff member, died of cancer in May 1992. A fund was established in his memory, and friends and family contributed more than $12,000 to it. Over time, other individuals donated the remaining money to build the entire house.

The National Association of Home Builders agreed to build a house in memory of Bill Gray, Jr., one of its young staffers who had died of cancer in 1992. (This house was co-sponsored by Meredith Corporation and Chevy Trucks.)

Other house sponsors included the Tog Shop, an outstanding local industry; the John S. and James L. Knight Foundation (two houses);

Weyerhaeuser Company; the United Methodist Committee on Relief; Bell-South Telecommunications, Inc.; Georgia Power Company; Square D Company; Trammel Crow Residential Company; John Wieland Homes, Inc.; Alphawave Designs; National Gypsum Company; Deloitte & Touche; Black & Decker Corporation; and Lutheran Brotherhood.

After all twenty sponsorships were secured, we were contacted by MBNA America Bank, N.A., a fine credit card company headquartered in Maryland. Since no additional sponsorships were available, we decided MBNA could build the twenty-first house as the first of the next 20,000 houses! During the week of blitz-building, the company employees installed a large sign in front of their house that proclaimed, "Breaking the Barrier—20,001!"

In December 1992, a "test" house was built in the little town of DeSoto, ten miles east of Americus, as our traditional Christmas house. It was finished on schedule in just five days. We felt ready for the big blitz-build in April.[3]

During Holy Week, over 700 volunteers came from forty-four states and the District of Columbia, Canada, England, New Zealand, Honduras, and Australia for the blitz-building. They were joined by over 400 local volunteer builders and support people from Americus and Sumter County.

The project was a huge success. Jimmy and Rosalynn Carter worked on Monday, April 5, the day of the most dramatic building when the walls were erected, the roofs were attached, and the doors and windows installed. Actress Jane Fonda also joined us for that exciting first day of building. All houses were completed on schedule and the families moved in on Saturday, April 10, amidst great rejoicing.

Local, state, and national media coverage included features on national radio, CNN television, and many other TV stations; major stories also ran in the *Atlanta Journal/Constitution*, *USA Today*, and numerous other newspapers across the country.

As this book is going to press in early 1994, the pace of Sumter County Initiative's work is steadily increasing. Thirty houses will be built in Americus during the week of June 13–17 as our 30/30,000 Project, an "encore" to the highly successful 20/20,000 Project. (The thirtieth house will be the 30,000th built by Habitat for Humanity.) In total, Habitat will build at least fifty houses in Americus and Sumter County in 1994. Other groups will erect or renovate several more. In 1995 and in succeeding years until the end of the decade, Habitat, the City of Americus, and other organizations—principally Christian Rebuilders—will build and renovate sixty to eighty houses a year.

As poverty housing is being eliminated in Americus and Sumter County, Georgia, by the year 2000, so it is being eliminated in the Yure

River basin in northern Honduras. That international affiliate has been linked to the Sumter County Initiative through Habitat's tithing program so that all poverty housing can be wiped out in that area, too, within the same period.[4] By early 1994, 215 houses had been completed there. The plan is to continue building 100 houses per year until the year 2000 when we project we will have built houses for all those living in substandard housing in that part of Honduras.

A light has been set ablaze in south Georgia (and in northern Honduras), and it is burning brightly. Problems exist, to be sure, and always will; but we know that God has called us to this task, and we move on in faith that the God we serve is greater than any obstacle.

Special events like the 20/20,000 and 30/30,000 Projects, daring programs like the Sumter County Initiative, blitz-building with President Carter, and other such dramatic endeavors are highly visible components of our strategy to eliminate substandard housing and homelessness. All are a part of "the theology of the hammer." Such events bring people together and energize them to get the job done.

The final dimension of "the theology of the hammer" is the realization that sufficient resources exist for solving the problem of poverty housing and homelessness. Rocks, sand, cement, lumber, and other materials needed for house building are in abundant supply, along with the knowledge of how to build. Only the will to solve the problem is missing. God has chosen us, we believe, to be His instruments to put this issue on the hearts of people in churches, civic clubs, businesses, foundations, governments, and other organizations in such a way that effective action will be taken to solve this very solvable problem. "The theology of the hammer" proclaims that, with God, all things are possible, and that certainly includes a world without shacks and homeless people. Everybody made in the image of God, and that's the whole crowd, ought to have a decent place to live and on terms they can afford to pay.

Notes

[1]For a full discussion of biblical economics, see chapter 8, "The Economics of Jesus," in my book, *Love in the Mortar Joints*.

[2]You will read more about this rapidly proliferating movement in chapter 8.

[3]Another Christmas house was built in DeSoto in 1993. See the dramatic "before and after" photographs on page 20.

[4]For a full discussion of Habitat's tithing program, see chapter 4.

Millard Fuller speaking at ground breaking for the 30/30,000 Project in Americus, GA, Sunday afternoon, February 13, 1994. (Photo by Dennis Meola)

BEFORE AND AFTER—No more shacks! is the motto of the Habitat for Humanity. This rundown shack (above) in DeSoto, GA, near Americus was torn down, and a new Habitat house (below) took its place, providing decent shelter and hope to another partner family.

Chapter 2

Matching Word with Deed

"The theology of the hammer" is bringing together all kinds of people, churches, and institutions to build and renovate houses for needy families; it is also bringing us closer to God as we work with one another. Well-known Christian author Henri J. M. Nouwen reminds us that the original meaning of the word "theology" was "union with God in prayer."[1] "The theology of the hammer" joins the proclamation of our faith with the living out and working out of that faith. It is a matching of word and deed.

In his classic book, *A Theology for the Social Gospel*, Walter Rauschenbusch wrote, "When the progress of humanity creates new tasks . . . or new problems . . . theology must connect these with the old fundamentals of our faith and make them Christian tasks and problems."[2]

I believe our human progress has, indeed, created the new task of eliminating poverty housing and homelessness. And, this task can be accomplished if, and only if, we develop a theology that connects the task with the old fundamentals of faith and makes it our Christian task to solve.

As Henri Nouwen points out, that theology means union with God in prayer. He asserts: "It is of vital importance to reclaim the mystical aspect of theology so that every word spoken, every advice given, and every strategy developed can come from a heart that knows God intimately."[3] But, having prayed and come to an understanding of God's will, there is the imperative to act.

Rauschenbusch taught that a theology that asserts a union of religion and righteous life and action takes religion to a higher plane. Here are his words:

> It is clear that our Christianity is most Christian when religion and ethics are viewed as inseparable elements of the same single-minded and whole-hearted life, in which the consciousness of God and the consciousness of humanity blend completely. Any new movement in theology, which emphatically asserts the union of religion and ethics, is likely to be a wholesome and Christianizing force in Christian thought.
>
> The social gospel is of that nature. It plainly concentrates religious interest on the great ethical problems of social life. It scorns the tithing of mint, anise, and cumin, at which the Pharisees are still busy, and insists on getting down to the weightier matters of God's law, to justice and mercy. It ties up religion not only with duty, but with big duty that stirs the soul with religious feeling and throws it back on God for help. The non-ethical

practices and beliefs in historical Christianity nearly all center on the winning of heaven and immortality. On the other hand, the kingdom of God can be established by nothing except righteous life and action.[4]

Righteous life and action are central to a full-bodied faith and certainly to "the theology of the hammer." Unfortunately, many people act as if Jesus had taught that the first and greatest commandment is this: Thou shall go to church. And, the second is like it: Thou shall try to get others to go to church.

Of course, Jesus never taught any such thing. We are admonished "Let us not give up meeting together" (Heb 10:25). Worship services, Sunday School, and other religious gatherings are important, but they are not the *end* of true religion. Such gatherings should serve to motivate, inspire, and equip us for devotion and service to the Lord and to needy humanity in the world.

Jesus summarized very clearly the priorities of the kingdom of God when he answered the question, "Teacher, which is the greatest commandment in the Law?" He responded in unequivocal words about the very essence of unadorned religion, clear and right to the heart of the matter:

> Love the Lord your God with all your heart and with all your soul, and with all your mind. This is the first and greatest commandment. And the second is like it: Love your neighbor as yourself. All the Law and the Prophets hang on these two commandments. (Matt 22:36-40)

This bringing together of the love of God and love of neighbor is stressed throughout scripture. The spoken word, praising and expressing love of God, is one-dimensional and incomplete without the expression of love to people—the deed. Moses, for example, was said to be a man "of power in words and deeds" (Acts 7:22). The same words were used to describe Jesus: "mighty in deed and word in the sight of God and all the people" (Luke 24:19). Mark 6:30 tells us, "The apostles gathered around Jesus and reported to Him all they had done and taught." The Apostle John connected word and deed with this beautiful proclamation:

> This is how we know what love is: Jesus Christ laid down his life for us. And we ought to lay down our lives for our brothers. If anyone has material possessions and sees his brother in need but has no pity on him, how can the love of God be in him? Dear children, let us not love with words or tongue but with actions and in truth. (1 John 3:16-18)

My colleague Walden Howard, former *Faith at Work* magazine editor and the "founding father" of Habitat for Humanity on Maryland's Lower Shore, addresses this subject in terms of faith and action. He writes,

> One aspect of faith is a belief system. As Christians there are certain identifying beliefs that we hold. We may differ on non-essentials, but there are certain essential beliefs about God, ourselves, and the world that we hold in common, though; as Clarence Jordan taught us, our true belief system may be other than what we profess. Belief, he explained, came from the Old English words for "by life."
>
> In Hebrews 10:22 the writer speaks of "full assurance of faith." Faith, then, is at its root trust. God wants most of all that we trust Him, however clear or unclear our belief system may be. Nothing describes a person of faith more than basic trust. We act either out of trust or fear. Hence, Jesus came not so much to save us from our sins as to save us from our fears.
>
> Later on in the book of Hebrews, the writer says that faith is also vision. It is "the conviction of things not seen"; it is "seeing him who is invisible." Faith sees and acts on a different reality than meets the human eye. It sees possibilities rather than problems; it sees what God has in mind, regardless of outward circumstances.
>
> But faith, finally, is action. The whole eleventh chapter of Hebrews is the story of those who trusted God enough and saw what God wanted them to do clearly enough to act on it. The vision is not faith until it is put into action.
>
> So, faith is fourfold. It is belief, trust, vision, action.[5]

Some people equate word with evangelism and deed with social action. My friend Clyde Tilley, whose theological perspectives I have already acknowledged in the introduction, says,

> Evangelism is the word-method by which we communicate God's love to the world. Social action is the deed-method by which we communicate God's love to the world. Expressing God's love is not a matter of either word or deed; it is a matter of both word and deed. . . . It is a matter of "show and tell," perhaps most effectively in that order. Evangelism that endeavors to witness by word, and social action that endeavors to serve by deed, must be integrated into the obedient lifestyle of Christian discipleship.[6]

Clyde goes on to write that some Christian groups are primarily concerned with getting people ready for "mansions in the sky by and by" but are quite content to leave them in shacks here and now. Other groups urgently want to build and renovate houses for the poor, but have little or no concern for the eternal home for the people they are helping or even for their own personal relationship with Christ.

Clarence Jordan talked about this matter of word versus deed in terms of "incarnational evangelism." He believed that the only authentic method of proclaiming God's word—that is, evangelism—was incarnationally, that is to say, by the word becoming deed. He pointed out that God chose that method of evangelizing when God sent the Son into the world. The word became flesh in the person of Jesus of Nazareth. God "wrote" His message on a man and delivered the message that way. Hence, Clarence concluded that the method of evangelism of the New Testament is to confront people with a visible word.

Clarence was adamant that words alone were never enough. With his biting wit he wrote,

> The word became a sermon and was later expanded into a book, and the book sold well and inspired other books until of the making of books there was no end. And the world died in darkness and was buried in the theological library.[7]

In short, words alone just do not deliver the message.

St. Francis of Assisi certainly agreed that mere words are not enough. Indeed, he is quoted as having said, "Preach the gospel at all times. If necessary, use words!"

Albert Schweitzer, too, acknowledged the inadequacy of words alone when he wrote about his decision to become a missionary doctor:

> I wanted to be a doctor so that I might be able to work without having to talk. For years I had been giving of myself in words, and it was with joy that I had followed the calling of theological teacher and preacher. But this new form of activity would consist not in preaching the religion of love, but in practicing it.[8]

Jesus told his disciples they were "salt," but he warned them not to become "tasteless." He said they were "light," but that they must never allow the "light" to be "put under a basket." Rather, he taught that their "light" must be seen through their deeds: "Let your light shine before men that they may see your good deeds and praise your Father in heaven" (Matt 5:16).

In his account of the final judgment in Matthew, Jesus made abundantly clear the importance of *deeds*. In fact, in that dramatic story, only the deeds count:

> For I was hungry and you gave me something to eat, I was thirsty, and you gave me something to drink, I was a stranger and you invited me in, I needed clothes and you clothed me, I was sick, and you looked after me, I was in prison, and you came to visit me. Then the righteous will answer him, "Lord, when did we see you hungry and feed you, or thirsty and give you something to drink? When did we see you a stranger and invite you in, or needing clothes and clothe you? When did we see you sick or in prison and

go to visit you?" The king will reply, "I tell you the truth, whatever you did for one of the least of these brothers of mine, you did for me." (25:35-40)

John the Baptist, the forerunner of Jesus, spoke with equal clarity about the importance of the deed in one's religious life. Clarence Jordan said that John had not invested in Norman Vincent Peale's "Power of Positive Thinking." Instead, he was heavily oriented toward negative preaching. His method was to "hang them over the edge and singe their eyebrows!" Hear him thunder away:

> John said to the crowds coming out to be baptized by him, "You brood of vipers! Who warned you to flee from the coming wrath? Produce fruit in keeping with repentance. And do not begin to say to yourselves, 'We have Abraham as our father.' For I tell you that out of these stones God can raise up children for Abraham. The ax is already at the root of the trees, and every tree that does not produce good fruit will be cut down and thrown into the fire." "What should we do then?" the crowd asked. John answered, "The man with two tunics should share with him who has none, and the one who has food should do the same." (Luke 3:7-11)

Isaiah, who preached hundreds of years before either John the Baptist or Jesus, proclaimed a message that was amazingly similar. Reaching out to those in need, doing something to help the hungry, the homeless, the naked, was the very essence of true and pure religion. It was the *sine qua non* of righteousness. He expressed himself in terms of "the fast" that is pleasing to God:

> Is not this the kind of fasting I have chosen:
>   to loose the chains of injustice
>   and untie the cords of the yoke,
>   to set the oppressed free
>   and break every yoke?
> Is it not to share your food with the hungry
>   and to provide the poor wanderer with shelter—
> when you see the naked, to clothe him,
>   and not to turn away from your own flesh and blood?
> Then your light will break forth like the dawn,
>   and your healing will quickly appear;
> then your righteousness will go before you,
>   and the glory of the Lord will be your rear guard.
> Then you will call, and the Lord will answer;
>   you will cry for help, and he will say: "Here am I."
> If you do away with the yoke of oppression,
>   with the pointing finger and malicious talk,
> and if you spend yourselves in behalf of the hungry
>   and satisfy the needs of the oppressed,

then your light will rise in darkness,
 and your night will become like noonday.
The Lord will guide you always;
 he will satisfy your needs in a sun-scorched land
  and will strengthen your frame.
You will be like a well-watered garden,
 like a spring whose waters never fail.
Your people will rebuild the ancient ruins
 and will raise up the age-old foundations;
you will be called Repairer of Broken Walls,
 Restorer of Streets with Dwellings. (58:6-12)

"The theology of the hammer" embraces wholeheartedly the idea that the love of God and love of man must be blended. The word and the deed must come together. One without the other is devoid of meaning.

We build houses in Habitat for Humanity for the good of needy families and our theology is that of the hammer. We know well that "Unless the Lord builds the house, its builders labor in vain" (Ps 127:1). We know equally well that talking and praying alone will never dig the foundation, nor will piety by itself put up the walls. Only the powerful combination of the word and deed can get the job done.

When word and deed are blended, however, there is often a startling result. Let me share with you three stories that illustrate the amazing results of faith and work coming together.

The first story is from Scranton, Pennsylvania. Judith Kosydar, president of Habitat for Humanity of Lackawanna County, tells about the first big work day on her affiliate's first project, the rehabilitation of an old dilapidated house. The people assembled on a cold January morning and, following a moving devotional service, they were ready for work. Judith describes the scene:

> Human work chains expanded from the second floor, down the stairs, and outside to the dumpster—handing the trash from one pair of arms to another. Within one hour, I realized that the first trailer-size dumpster was not large enough, so I immediately got another to the site. By three o'clock, in only four hours, over 125 volunteers completely gutted every room in the house to the studs and had filled two trailer-size dumpsters with nearly ten tons of debris! What happened that day was nothing less than a transformation of people into partners.
>
> A volunteer collected the scrap metal and returned in his pickup to give Habitat the fixty-six dollars he had received from recycling it. A restaurant owner heard the live radio coverage and came delivering hot coffee and sandwiches. A shut-in from my church came to see what this new mission endeavor was all about.
>
> That day we were one body, united despite our socio-cultural or religious differences. It was faith turned into action.

The second story is from the mountains of West Virginia, in Pendleton County, where Almost Heaven Habitat for Humanity is located. This very productive affiliate, which was started by and continues under the leadership of Kirk Lyman Barner, had built and renovated twenty-five houses and repaired another forty by the end of 1993.

Located in an economically poor area, the folks in Pendleton County rely heavily on work camps from other parts of the country. One such work camp, from Connecticut, went there in early 1992. In that work group were Judy and Cal Crabill, long-time and very dedicated Habitat partners. Judy wrote movingly about their experiences:

> I witnessed the Holy Spirit change CEO's into ditch diggers and heard them declare that nothing the next week could be as good as "now." I watched in disbelieving awe as beautiful socialites shared one closet-size, makeshift, bathroom with twenty others and now, at home again, tell me they miss the curtain partitions.
>
> It was cold, less than twenty degrees some days, and snowing! But the cold and snow did not slow the work. A fire-barrel served to warm our hands every forty-five minutes. Then, it was back to sawing, hammering, roofing, framing, and pouring cement. Hot soup and tiny, close quarters insured a bonding and a metamorphosis that cannot be explained except in the heart.
>
> Despite our disparate backgrounds, we met on level ground as brothers and sisters, searching for God. And, we found Him! Oh! How we found Him!
>
> On Friday evening we invited the local folks to our house (or was it a "retired" chicken coop?) for a hymn sing. They started coming an hour early. As each one slipped through the doorway, the level of excitement grew and the singing became more exuberant. By the time the last person arrived, we were all higher than astronauts on a space ship. The building was crowded with noisy joy.
>
> The whole experience was a screaming success! Wealthy Weston, Connecticut, met poor Circleville, West Virginia, in Almost Heaven. And now some wonder who's got it right! One certain fact is that none of us will ever be the same.

The third story is from the other side of the country, in California. In early August 1992, the United Methodists of northern California and Nevada convened "Jubilee '92" in Humboldt County. This gathering brought together over 1,400 people from United Methodist churches for a five-day conference.

Usually, such meetings consist solely of workshops, seminars, Bible study, and plenary sessions—all concerned with the "word" side of faith. At the "Jubilee '92" gathering, however, attendees were given the option of helping to build two houses in partnership with Humboldt Habitat for Humanity. All the United Methodist churches involved raised all the money needed to build the houses, and more than 200 people volunteered to do the actual building.

Two families were chosen by the family selection committee of Humboldt Habitat to receive the houses. The foundations were poured ahead of time, and all needed materials were placed on site. I was invited to participate in the last day of the event, which included visiting both building sites and addressing the entire conference in the evening.

When I arrived, I was briefed about what had transpired at both the conference and in the building activity and was then taken on a tour of the two work sites. Our first stop was in the little town of Manila. There, a modest but beautiful house was nearing completion for a single woman who had been living in a decaying mobile home. The woman, Nelda Rose, was ecstatic about her house. She smiled so broadly as we talked that I thought her lips might split! She was absolutely joy incarnate because she was getting a new house.

Next, we drove a few miles to McKinleyville, another small town where the second house was being built. When we walked into the yard of the house, a young woman came running toward me. She leaped into my arms and gave me a big hug. Then, she turned loose, stepped back, and tried to speak to me. No words came. She stood sobbing and wiping the tears from her eyes. After a few awkward moments, she walked away.

Garvin Jabusch walked up. A dedicated Christian and a skilled builder, Garvin was the team leader for the house. He told me, "Millard, that is Joanne Waters. She's the homeowner of this house. Don't worry about her crying. She's been crying the whole four days we've been here." He told me how Joanne had said she had not expected to cry as we raised each wall of her house, but this seemed to happen anyway.

Garvin shared with me her story. She was a single mother, with two boys, aged five and twelve. Limited by only a high school diploma, the best job she could find was waitress at a local restaurant, paying minimum wage. She and her sons had been living in a small automobile garage. Humboldt Habitat had learned about her plight and had chosen her family to have that new house. Garvin said she was simply overwhelmed by the prospect of moving out of that garage and into a good house.

He went on to tell me about something that happened at the end of the first work day:

> We got up the walls and trusses, and we put on the plyboard and felt paper for the roof. The doors and windows were installed, and we got set up for siding and shingling to be done the next day. After the crew had quit for the day, Joanne and I were alone, picking up tools and straightening up. When we were done, we sat on the bare floor in her living room, talking. With tears

streaming down her cheeks, she said, "I just can't believe this is happening to me. It's a miracle."

That evening, I addressed the assembly of "Jubilee '92." Beside me stood the two women. Nelda was all smiles and full of joy. She talked openly and with enthusiasm and appreciation about her new Habitat house. Joanne just heaved great sobs. But both women communicated. Their words and emotion profoundly affected everyone present. The offering, all for Habitat for Humanity, was over $11,000!

A couple of weeks later, I received a long letter from Leon McDuff. "Duffy," as he is known to his family and friends, had organized the blitz-build for "Jubilee '92." He was writing to give me a report. Duffy said that both families moved into their homes on schedule and that all those involved—the volunteers, the families, Humboldt Habitat people, and church leaders—were very pleased and happy about the pioneering project.

He went on to say that Joanne had approached project leaders after moving in to say that she continued to be overwhelmed by what had happened to her. She found it hard to believe that total strangers would descend on a work site and build a house for her and her boys. She said she did not know there were people like that in the world.

Joanne confessed that she desired to have in her life what she saw in those people. She said that she had briefly attended a church years earlier but had dropped out. She wanted to learn more about the beliefs of the United Methodist Church. She wondered if the love and caring she had felt so strongly that week were representative of the whole church. Soon, she and her boys started attending a local United Methodist church.

Joanne was evangelized in the deepest sense. Fusion of the *word* of God with the *deed* of God delivered a message to her heart.

Habitat for Humanity does not build houses to convert the new homeowners. Many Habitat homeowners are already strong Christians long before their houses are built. Others are not Christians and do not become Christians because they get a Habitat house.

Salvation does not come from Habitat for Humanity. Salvation does not come from me or from any other individual. Salvation comes only from God. Our task is to love and to proclaim faith, in both word and deed, and leave the results to the Lord.

Something wonderful happens when word and deed come together, though. It is a joy, and it is God's truth. As Henri Nouwen tells us, theology is about God and people coming together in prayer. "The theology of the hammer" is, likewise, about bringing God and people together and about bringing people closer to one another in work, study, play, and all other activities of life. As the deed gets closer to the word,

God gets closer to us. The results are always wonderful—and sometimes spectacular!

Notes

[1]Henri J. M. Nouwen, *In the Name of Jesus* (New York: Crossroad, 1989) 20.

[2]Walter Rauschenbusch, *A Theology for the Social Gospel* (Nashville: Abingdon, 1945) 7.

[3]Nouwen, 30.

[4]Rauschenbusch, 14-15.

[5]From personal correspondence from Walden Howard to Millard Fuller.

[6]W. Clyde Tilley, "Word and Deed: In Search of a Balance," (unpublished manuscript, 1993).

[7]Dallas Lee, ed., *The Substance of Faith and Other Sermons by Clarence Jordan* (New York: Association Press, 1972) 33.

[8]Albert Schweitzer, *Out of My Life and Thought* (New York: Henry Holt and Company, 1949) 92.

Chapter 3

A Theology of Enough

A rich man in Atlanta recently built for himself and his family a huge house on a large parcel of land. The amenities included an attached carriage house, a swimming pool, a lake, extensive flower gardens, and many other wonderful features. People compared this awesome layout to the palace in Versailles, France. When asked why he built such an extravagant place he exclaimed, "Because I'm a born-again Christian and I wanted to glorify God."

Is God glorified when a family builds for itself housing that is vastly in excess of what the legitimate needs are for that family? Or, is God glorified more when a wealthy family exercises restraint, builds more modestly for its needs, and uses the excess funds to build additional modest houses for less fortunate families?

What do you think? What does the Bible have to say on this subject? Reflect on these pertinent words from Deuteronomy:

> Be careful that you do not forget the Lord your God, failing to observe his commands, his laws, and his decrees that I am giving you this day. Otherwise, when you eat and are satisfied, when you build fine houses and settle down, and when your herds and your flocks grow large and your silver and gold increase and all you have is multiplied, then your heart will become proud, and you will forget the Lord your God. (8:11-14)

Isaiah minced no words in railing against those who want more and more, bigger and bigger, until they crowd everybody else out:

> Woe to you who add house to house and join field to field, till no space is left and you live alone in the land. The Lord Almighty has declared in my hearing: "Surely the great houses will become desolate, the fine mansions left without occupants." (5:8-9)

Amos was even sharper in his condemnation of the rich and their big houses:

> "I will tear down the winter house
>   along with the summer house;
> the houses adorned with ivory will be destroyed
> and the mansions will be demolished,"
>   declares the Lord. . . .
> Therefore, though you have built stone mansions,
>   you will not live in them;

though you have planted lush vineyards,
   you will not drink their wine.
For I know how many are your offenses
   and how great your sins.
You oppress the righteous and take bribes
   and you deprive the poor of justice
      in the courts. (3:15; 5:11b-12)

Jeremiah also heaped condemnation on the person who builds a roomy house but does not concern himself with justice and righteousness. Then, he concluded with a clear admonition that "defending the cause of the poor and needy" is what it means to know the Lord:

Woe to him who builds his palace by unrighteousness, his upper rooms by injustice, making his countrymen work for nothing, not paying them for their labor. He says, "I will build myself a great palace with spacious upper rooms." So he makes large windows in it, panels it with cedar, and decorates it in red. Does it make you a king to have more and more cedar? Did not your father have food and drink? He did what was right and just, so all went well with him. He defended the cause of the poor and needy, and so all went well. "Is that not what it means to know me?" declares the Lord. (22:13-16)

Jack Abrams of Habitat for Humanity of Manasota in Sarasota, Florida, shared a remarkable story with me about a rich man who did have a heart of concern for the poor. The episode started with a letter I received from a man who was living in a very deficient garage apartment in Nokomis, a town near Sarasota. I forwarded the letter to John Schaub, president of Manasota Habitat, and asked him to investigate the matter. John passed the letter along to Jack, who related what happened:

My wife, Audrey, and I approached the address and saw that it was a large estate right on the bay. Obviously, only a wealthy man could afford such an expansive estate, and our righteous indignation jumped to the fore. We were prepared to ask some searching questions concerning his negligence in furnishing proper living conditions for the poor man who lived in the apartment above the garage.

As we drove up the long winding driveway, a man came out of the imposing house. I introduced myself and explained why we were there. Before I could ask the searching questions we had so carefully prepared, the gentleman informed us that the man who had written the letter of complaint had moved out before he, the present owner, had moved in.

Realizing this was an excellent opportunity to do some missionary work for Habitat, I described our activities in the southern part of the county. The gentleman had heard of Habitat but did not know there was a local affiliate. I asked if I could come back and bring some literature about our work. He invited us to do so.

We drove home and returned immediately with the material. The result was a $10,000 donation for a house we were planning to build in Nokomis only about a mile from his estate.

That house has subsequently been built for a family that was living in a run-down trailer. One of the children of that family was lodged in a closet in the trailer. Their new house is now complete and the little boy who slept in the closet has a nice big room. He hugs me constantly whenever I visit.

We need more rich people (and middle income people!) such as the man in this story. Unfortunately, not all wealthy people have that kind of a loving, caring, and sharing heart.

Jesus repeatedly warned the rich about their neglect of the poor. He clearly stated that the likelihood of a rich person getting into the kingdom of God is about as remote as that of a camel going through the eye of a needle. He told the powerful story of the rich man who did not help Lazarus, a beggar who was covered with sores and who lay at his gate. When the two men eventually died, the angels carried Lazarus to Abraham's side and the rich man went to hell. According to the story, the rich man's sin was simply that of wealth and callous unconcern for the poor.

Jesus also told a parable about a rich man who filled up his existing barns with abundant crops. Reflecting on his excess, the prosperous man decided to tear down the old barns and build bigger ones. The story, I submit, is equally applicable to houses. Hear these eternally relevant words of our Lord:

> "Watch out! Be on your guard against all kinds of greed; a man's life does not consist in the abundance of his possessions." And he told them this parable: "The ground of a certain rich man produced a good crop. He thought to himself, 'What shall I do? I have no place to store my crops.' Then he said, 'This is what I'll do: I will tear down my barns and build bigger ones, and there I will store all my grain and my goods. And I'll say to myself, "You have plenty of good things laid up for many years. Take life easy; eat, drink and be merry." ' "But God said to him, 'You fool! This very night your life will be demanded from you. Then who will get what you have prepared for yourself?' " This is how it will be with anyone who stores up things for himself, but is not rich toward God. (Luke 12:15-21)

I was raised in a Christian home in the small east Alabama cotton mill town of Lanett. Our family faithfully attended Sunday School and church. I learned the teachings of the Bible about wealth. I memorized one of the central teachings of Jesus: that one should, "seek first his kingdom and his righteousness, and all these things will be given to you as well" (Matt 6:33). I knew that Jesus had said it was very difficult for a rich person to inherit the kingdom of God. I also knew that Jesus said, "With God, all things are possible" (Matt 19:26).

At an early age, I decided that I wanted to be a wealthy person. At the same time I wanted to remain faithful to my Christian upbringing. My ambition was to be a Christian rich man. The Bible said so very clearly that such would be difficult, but I did not mind a challenge! I would just have to keep things in proper perspective, seeking to do God's will first and foremost and then going after the other things.

This all seemed very logical. I began my business career even in elementary school: fattening and selling a pig. I went on to raising and selling more pigs, then chickens, rabbits, and cattle. I engaged in some other business ventures in high school and in undergraduate school at Auburn University. In law school at the University of Alabama, I met a fellow student named Morris Dees, Jr. The two of us formed a company that began to make some significant money. Over an eight-year period we developed the company that was eventually named Fuller and Dees Marketing Group, Inc. The last five of those eight years were spent in Montgomery, Alabama, where we had a law office and headquarters for our young company.

As time went on, I spent more and more time working. I had married Linda Caldwell of Tuscaloosa, Alabama, in my senior year of law school. At first, we were very happy; but, after moving to Montgomery, I practically made her a widow by being virtually married to the company. We drifted apart, despite the fact that I was buying more and more things for Linda and myself. She had more clothes and shoes than she could get into the closets. She had a full-time maid to clean the house and help take care of the two children born during the first three years of our marriage. Linda was continuing her education at nearby Huntingdon College.

We bought a spacious old brick house in the Cloverdale section of the city, a new Lincoln Continental automobile, and a cabin on Lake Martin, near Wetumpka, Alabama. My partner and I started buying land; soon we owned 2,000 acres with cattle, horses, and many fishing lakes. Not satisfied with the house Linda and I owned, I bought a twenty-acre lot and hired an architect to draw plans for a much larger house.

The treasurer of our company told me one day that a newly produced financial statement showed that I, personally, was worth $1,000,000. I responded that my next goal was $10,000,000.

Before I could reach that new goal, however, Linda precipitated a crisis. Sitting on the edge of our king-sized bed one Saturday evening, she told me that she did not love me anymore. She announced that she needed to leave town and to think about our future or decide if we even had one together. I was shaken to my foundation.

The complete story of this tumultuous time in our lives is told in depth in my earlier books *Bokotola* and *Love In the Mortar Joints*,[1] but just let me recount here that we were eventually reconciled in an emotional reunion in New York City. A decision was made there to sell my interest in the company and give all the money away. We wanted to make ourselves poor again in order to rekindle our own love relationship and to put ourselves right with God. We both realized that we had strayed far from God's path for our lives. In a truly miraculous way, God led us to Koinonia Farm near Americus, Georgia, and to our magnificent encounter with Clarence Jordan.

Someone once said that when the student is ready to learn the teacher appears. Clarence Jordan was our teacher. He helped us to see the great power that possessions have over people. Our whole culture blares constantly that the totality of a person is the things he or she has. We even ask questions like, "Do you know what Mr. So-and-so is worth?" Everything is determined by one's monetary worth; nothing else counts.

Clarence once said that the emptier a person is on the inside, the more that person needs on the outside to compensate for that inward emptiness. As I more fully comprehended the great truthfulness of what my new friend was saying, the Bible came absolutely alive to me. I resonated, especially with scripture such as that found in 1 Timothy where the Apostle Paul was sharing with his young assistant about wealth and how it should be used:

> Command those who are rich in this present world not to be arrogant nor to put their hope in wealth, which is so uncertain, but to put their hope in God, who richly provides us with everything for our enjoyment. Command them to do good, to be rich in good deeds, and to be generous and willing to share. In this way they will lay up treasures for themselves as a firm foundation for the coming age, so that they may take hold of the life that is truly life. (1 Tim 6:17-19)

I was also struck by Paul's second letter to the Corinthians in which he talked about true riches and the need of those with an abundance to share with those who have too little so that there might be equality:

> For you know the grace of our Lord Jesus Christ, that though he was rich, yet for your sakes he became poor, so that you through his poverty might become rich. And here is my advice about what is best for you in this matter: Last year you were the first not only to give but also to have the desire to do so. Now finish the work, so that your eager willingness to do it may be matched by your completion of it, according to your means. For if the willingness is there, the gift is acceptable according to what one has, not according to what he does not have. Our desire is not that others might be relieved while you are hard pressed, but that there might be equality. At the present time your plenty will supply what they need, so that in turn their plenty will supply what you need. Then there will be equality, as it is

written: "He who gathered much did not have too much, and he who gathered little did not have too little." (8:9-15)

These passages, and many more like them found throughout the Bible, are all a part of "the theology of the hammer." God has put all that is needed on the earth—in human, natural, and financial resources—to solve completely the problems of poverty housing and homelessness.

One of the big impediments to solving the problem is that too few talented and wealthy people have a developed "theology of enough." They keep striving, struggling, and scrambling for more and more things for themselves and are too short-sighted and immature spiritually to see the futility of that type of grasping lifestyle.

The Bible is not the only book that contains dire warnings about putting trust in possessions and focusing earthly existence on incessant and insatiable acquisition. Materialism has been denounced by all the sages from Buddha to Muhammad, and every world religion is rife with warnings against the evils of excess. As Arnold Toynbee observed,

> These religious founders disagreed with each other in the pictures of what is the nature of the universe, the nature of the spiritual life, the nature of ultimate reality. But they all agreed in their ethical precepts. . . . They all said with one voice if we made material wealth our paramount aim, this would lead to disaster.[2]

Religious historian Robert Bellah confirmed and expanded upon what Toynbee said, stating:

> That happiness is to be attained through limitless material acquisition is denied by every religion and philosophy known to humankind, but is preached incessantly by every American television set.[3]

Everything in this world is passing away, including the T.V. set! The Bible is true when it says, "All men are like grass, and all their glory is like the flowers of the field; the grass withers and the flowers fall, but the word of the Lord stands forever" (1 Pet 1:24).

The only truly safe investment one can make in life is what is given away. That can never be taken from anyone. Everything else, eventually, will be taken by trickery, fraud, deception, bad management, poor investments, bankruptcy, ruinous divorce, theft, or death. You will be separated from your possessions, one way or the other!

Poet E. M. Poteat was surely right when he penned these poignant words:

Count up your conquests of sea and land,
Heap up your gold and hoard as you may.
All you can hold in your cold dead hand
Is what you have given away.

And so was the psalmist who wrote:

For all can see that wise men die;
The foolish and the senseless alike perish,
And leave their wealth to others.
Their tombs will remain their houses forever,
Their dwellings for endless generations,
Though they had named lands after themselves.
But man, despite his riches, does not endure;
He is like the beasts that perish.
This is the fate of those who trust in themselves,
And of their followers, who approve their sayings.
Like sheep they are destined for the grave,
And death will feed on them.
The upright will rule over them in the morning;
Their forms will decay in the grave,
Far from their princely mansions. (Ps 49:10-14)

True riches come from a life of service, a life committed to doing God's work in the world. Helping the poor is the most authentic service to God. Recall Jesus' message in Matthew 25 about feeding the hungry, giving water to the thirsty, inviting strangers in, providing clothing to the naked, and visiting the sick and those in prison.

Consider James 1:27, "True religion, pure and undefiled is this, to minister to the widow and orphans in their time of distress and to keep oneself unspoiled from the world."

Jesus' inaugural sermon announced, "The spirit of the Lord is on me, because he has anointed me to preach good news to the poor." During his entire ministry he went about doing good—feeding the hungry, healing the sick, restoring sight to the blind. How could we possibly miss the point?

Very early in the Bible, the author of Deuteronomy clearly stated how God wanted things to be "in the land the Lord was giving to His people."

There should be no poor among you, for in the land the Lord your God is giving you to possess as your inheritance, he will richly bless you. . . . If there is a poor man among your brothers in any of the towns of the land that the Lord your God is giving you, do not be hardhearted or tightfisted toward your poor brother. Rather be openhanded and freely lend him whatever he needs. . . . Give generously to him and do so without a grudging heart; then because of this the Lord your God will bless you in all your work and in everything you put your hand to. There will always be poor people in the land. Therefore I command you to be openhanded toward your brothers and toward the poor and needy in your land. (15:4, 7-8, 10-11)

Simply put, the message is that we must have a well developed "theology of enough." God's order of things holds no place for hoarding and greed. There are sufficient resources in the world for the needs of everybody, but not enough for the greed of even a significant minority.

The people of Habitat for Humanity in Guatemala surely know about generous sharing with those in need. They freely opened their hands to help a needy Habitat family. International Partners Charlie and Ruth Magill, serving in West Quetzaltenango, related the following:

> This is a sad story, but within it is the light of the theology of the hammer.
>
> Santiago Lopez, thirty-three years old, was not only a Habitat home-owner but also president of the local Habitat committee, president of the regional project, representative to the national Habitat for Humanity foundation, and member of the national directivo. He had all the Habitat philosophy in his heart as well as his head. He was also the father of three boys aged four, ten, and thirteen. He had finished high school three years before and was working half-time in a gas station and half-time as a compesino, or field worker.
>
> When Santiago died unexpectedly, his remaining mortgage was just over 2,700 quetzales, or $470. Marta, his widow, does not read or write. Her income from weaving might be five or six dollars per month—not enough to cover her monthly house payments of six dollars and sixty cents.
>
> There are eight Habitat projects in Guatemala, covering eighteen towns. The local committee in Ixchiguan, Departmento de San Marcos, sent a letter to the local committees of each project: "We want to tell you immediately that in our last meeting we were informed of the death of our companero Santiago Lopez, of Concepcion Chiquirichapa. Thinking about the difficult situation of his debts, we decided to help, soliciting from every Habitat homeowner two quetzales (forty cents) to be able to pay part of the debt of his house. For this, we ask each committee to do the same and to channel said help by way of the national office."
>
> When the committee in Concepcion Chiquirichapa received the letter from Ixchiguan, there was not a dry eye in the meeting. The newly elected president, Esteban Izara, remarked that he believes "Santiago is still alive. He is in my house. I would not have this house without his help." Others made similar comments, and after a long discussion, with many words of thanks for the sentiments expressed by the Ixchiguan committee, the homeowners voted unanimously to give two quetzales each. After the vote, there was a small discussion in the back of the room; then one homeowner asked: "Is this every month?"

In Christ's kingdom we are willing to give not only from our wealth, but also from our poverty. In the community of Habitat we are willing to help our neighbor's family without reservation—one time, or every month.

Habitat for Humanity is counting on all people—especially talented and wealthy people and richly blessed churches, companies, and other organizations—to come forward and to freely open their hands and hearts so that additional resources, both material and human, will be made available to rid the world of shacks and other poor housing and homelessness. For this to happen, many hearts and minds must go through a radical transformation. With God, all things truly are possible!

Linda and I now live modestly in Americus, Georgia. Our physical needs are being met, and our greatest joy is in helping others meet their basic needs rather than piling up more and more for ourselves. We think it is a better way to live.

Notes

[1]Millard Fuller, *Bokotola* (Piscataway NJ: New Century Publishers, 1977) and *Love in the Mortar Joints* (Clinton NJ: New Win Publishing, Inc., 1980).

[2]Alan Durning, *How Much Is Enough?* (New York: W. W. Norton, 1992) 143.

[3]Robert Bellah, *The Broken Covenant* (New York: Seabury Press, 1975).

Former HUD Secretary Jack Kemp, a member of the Habitat for Humanity International Board of Directors at work during a blitz-build in Atlanta. (Photo by Julie Lopez)

Chelsea Clinton, daughter of President and and Mrs. Clinton, helps frame a Habitat house.

Hammer in hand, Jack Kemp prepares for some work at a Habitat for Humanity building site in Atlanta.

Chapter 4

A New Manner of Thinking

Albert Einstein once opined that "the unleashed power of the atom has changed everything save our modes of thinking, thus we are drifting toward a catastrophe beyond comparison. We shall require a substantially new manner of thinking if mankind is to survive."[1]

Einstein, of course, was not the first person to say that we must have a new way of thinking. When Jesus emerged from the wilderness and launched his ministry, he cried out, "Change your whole way of thinking, for the new order of God's Spirit is confronting you and challenging you."

Clarence Jordan spoke often and eloquently about this dramatic announcement of Jesus. The King James Version of the Bible, he said, renders it as an anemic: "The kingdom of God is at hand; repent ye, and believe the gospel." Clarence correctly pointed out that, to most people, the word "repent" means feeling sorry for getting caught! The rendering of Jesus' announcement in Greek (the language of the original New Testament scriptures) is much deeper than that, however. In the fullest extent of Jesus' proclamation, he was saying that a total transformation of thinking is required. Old ideas must go, to be replaced with entirely new ones. Earthly, egocentric, selfish, narrow, nationalistic ways of thinking must be replaced with the expansive, inclusive, heavenly view and vision of God's new movement that is bursting upon us.

This new way of thinking is nothing more or less than God's way of thinking. How does one acquire that new way of thinking? Consider the well-worn term, "born again." Many people dismiss this idea as something from the right-wing fringe of the Christian faith—the so-called fundamentalists. I submit that this concept is central to acquiring a new way of thinking. In regard to the advice given to Nicodemus that he must be "born again," Clarence pointed out that what Jesus really told Nicodemus was that he must be *re-fathered* from above.[2] Because every earthly father passes along certain genes to the child when his sperm unites with the female egg, a child born as the result of that "fathering" will have a certain resemblance to his or her earthly father (and mother, too, of course).

In spiritual terms, God, the Father, is always available to impregnate a willing person with His ideas, with His very being. He never forces himself on anyone, however, because God is love; and love, by definition, does not coerce or force. A "re-fathering" only occurs when a person invites God into his or her life. At that point, a spiritual impregnation occurs and a "child of God" results. This new creature has a new way of thinking because he or she has been infused with God's nature. Everything has become new in this person's life, and all thinking patterns, values, and points of view are those of the heavenly Father.

God's chosen vehicle for producing children of God in the world is the church. Throughout scripture the church is portrayed in feminine terms. It is often called the bride of Christ. When the church is totally submissive and obedient to God, He is able to fill it with his genes; the result is children of God. On the other hand, when the church "goes a-whoring"—to use Clarence Jordan's term—and has relations with other lovers such as materialism, status, prestige, and so forth, children are born out of the loins of the church, but they are not truly children of God, and they do not have a new way of thinking. To the contrary, they have the identical thinking of the culture that produced them.[3]

I have always seen Habitat for Humanity as a servant of the church. In this ministry, we are neither a church nor a new kind of denomination. We are non-denominational and non-doctrinal, but the first purpose in our official Articles of Incorporation states clearly our Christian foundation. We are to "witness to the gospel of Jesus Christ throughout the world by working in cooperation with God's people in need to create a better habitat in which to live and work." Our desire is to help the church with its primary task of producing children of God in the world.

We work with Catholic and Protestant, Christian and other faith groups, black and white, sacred and secular, liberal and conservative, rich and poor, urban and rural, inner-city and suburban, government and private, business and civic, and innumerable other creative alliances. These wide-ranging partnerships are central to "the theology of the hammer."

We seek to bring individuals, churches, and other groups together to work on fulfilling our goal of eliminating poverty housing and homelessness from the face of the earth by building basic but adequate housing. As stated earlier, we want to put shelter on the hearts and minds of people in such a way that poverty housing and homelessness become socially, politically, morally, and religiously unacceptable in our nation and world. Our goal can only be realized, however, by a massive change of heart and a new way of thinking on the part of millions of people.

A vital aspect of our strategy is the creation of a church relations department whose task is to seek the support of the more than 350,000 churches in the United States; 30,000 in Canada; and the many thousands more around the world. The department is attempting to expand the thinking and to stimulate creative new approaches within these churches to help the members see their neighbors in a different light and to view those neighbors the same way God does.[4]

The Christian religion is expansive, and every local church should be expansive. The door should be eternally open and the invitation warm and genuine for those on the outside to enter. Love should characterize every church because God is love, and God should be the head of every church. No one should be excluded. What is the most effective way to invite people in? How can the church best extend the invitation to those on the outside—to those who feel left out, alienated, alone, or abandoned?

Preaching is important, of course, but, typically, the preaching is done in the church to those who are already members. Publications are printed and distributed, but many who should read the material do not receive it or, even if they do, do not read it. Messages are broadcast via radio and television, but, again, many who should hear are not tuned in.

At the end of Jesus' earthly ministry, he gave his followers a clear mandate to be expansive and to aggressively invite others into the fellowship:

> Go and make disciples of all nations, baptizing them in the name of the Father and of the Son and of the Holy Spirit, and teaching them to obey everything I have commanded you. And surely I will be with you always, to the very end of the age. (Matt 28:19-20)

My dream, from the outset of the ministry of Habitat for Humanity, has been for our work to be a new frontier in Christian missions. Habitat is not, has not been, and will not be an evangelistic organization that seeks to convert people to become Baptists, Catholics, Lutherans, Pentecostals, or whatever. Rather, we aggressively demonstrate God's love by all that we do. As our first official purpose states, we seek to witness to the gospel of Christ. We desire vital and dynamic partnerships with churches to do what no individual congregation or even an entire denomination can do alone. Habitat for Humanity is able to set a wonderful stage on which a church can let its light so shine that others can see its good works and glorify our father who is in heaven.

This work is a new mission field, an environment where people who normally do not work together can do so, to the betterment of the community and to the tangible benefit of those who are in need. Very often, so much more gets built than a house.

Let me tell you a story. The Uptown Habitat for Humanity of Chicago, under the able leadership of Jim Lundeen, learned that a single woman and her aged mother needed to have their house renovated. The younger woman owned the dilapidated place but lacked the financial resources to remedy the sad situation. Uptown Habitat agreed to do the renovation.

The women were too poor to afford to move elsewhere while the house was being redone, so, they stayed while volunteers maneuvered around them. After several months, as the renovation was nearing completion, the daughter came to Jim and confessed that she did not want the work to end.

"Why?" he asked. "You've had to live in such a mess for all these months. I thought you'd be happy that we were about finished!"

"No," she replied. "I will miss all my new friends who have been coming here to work. I've never experienced anything like this in my life. I am not a Christian, and I have been astounded that you people would help us like this. You have literally saved my mother's life. I am eternally grateful."

Soon thereafter, she asked one of the Habitat board members if she could become a Christian. She was so touched by what had happened to her and her mother. "Of course," was the reply, "but we did not do the work to convert you. We did it because we knew you needed help and because it is our understanding that God's love extends to everyone."

"I know," she replied, "but this is something I want to do. It was Jesus who brought these people to work together with us." The board member arranged for a pastor to counsel with her. Later, she was baptized and entered into fellowship with a local congregation. To me, this story dramatically illustrates the power of the new way of thinking that is needed to change the world for the better. Even in the ministry of Habitat for Humanity, we sometimes see people who want to limit their love and concern. At our headquarters in Americus, we have been contacted by people who only wanted to build houses for Christians. With that narrow way of thinking, the miracle in Chicago could never have occurred. God's love does extend to everybody. No one is left out. We promote this new way of thinking in our work, and it has revolutionary power.

The world is so incredibly divided, and so many groups promote narrow self-interest in various forms. We want to open up new horizons and challenge old assumptions.

Countless thousands of people love their immediate families—their wives or husbands, their children, and, usually their mothers, fathers, brothers, sisters, uncles, aunts, and some few other relatives who are not too far removed in kinship. They also probably have some kind of limited concern for a next-door neighbor or a friend at work. Beyond that, the world is too big and too complicated to consider.

Another group, still large, but not so big as the first one, has a more inclusive scope of love and concern for its extended family; these people also have a concern for their neighborhood or town, if not too large.

A third group, sizeable but smaller than the second one, has a concern that embraces people like themselves, perhaps people of their own race, or even the entire nation—especially if the nation is under some sort of real or perceived threat.

A fourth group, smaller still, has a concern for fellow Methodists or fellow evangelicals, or brother and sister charismatics, or maybe even fellow Christians in general, including those beyond regional or national boundaries.

The smallest group has a concern for the whole world: immediate family, neighbors, friends, fellow Presbyterians or Mennonites, the nation, the world, friends, other Christians, liberals, conservatives, Muslims, Hindus, even enemies. All barriers are down and the world is their neighborhood. People in this group resonate with the words in the immortal poem of Charles Edwin Markham entitled, "Outwitted."

> He drew a circle that shut me out,
>   Heretic, rebel a thing to flout.
> But love and I had a wit to win.
>   We drew a circle that took him in.

In which group do you think Jesus best fits? Consider his story of the Good Samaritan.

A lawyer wanted to know what he must do to justify himself, so he asked Jesus. Jesus answered, as was often his custom, with questions, "What is written in the Law? How do you read it?" (Luke 10:26).

The man replied, "Love the Lord your God with all your heart and with all your soul and with all your strength and with all your mind, and love your neighbor as yourself."

"You have answered correctly," Jesus replied. "Do this and you will live."

The man asked for clarification. "And who is my neighbor?"

Jesus then began this story:

"A man was going down from Jerusalem to Jericho, when he fell into the hands of robbers. They stripped him of his clothes, beat him, and went away, leaving him half dead."

Jesus went on to tell how a priest came by but did not stop. Likewise, another religious man, a Levite, passed by on the other side without offering to help. Then came a Samaritan, a man of another race, another religion, another culture. He stopped and rendered emergency assistance, which included taking the wounded man to an inn. Not only did he give immediate help, but he also paid the bill and left the robbery victim in the care of a responsible person with a promise to return and pay even more, if needed.

Jesus concluded the powerful story with the eternal question, "Which of these three do you think was a neighbor to the man who fell into the hands of robbers?"

The lawyer replied, "The one who had mercy on him." And Jesus said to him, "Go and do likewise."

The challenge is to get more and more people to think and act like the Samaritan in this story. The need is for a huge number of people all across the land and around the world to take down the barriers in their minds and hearts and to see the world as their neighborhood.

Each local Habitat affiliate in the United States, Canada, Australia, New Zealand, the United Kingdom, Poland, Hungary, or other developed countries is expected to give ten percent (the biblical tithe) of the money that is raised locally for building houses in developing countries.[5] A solemn covenant is signed by each such group, assenting to the expectation of contributing this ten percent of locally raised money to build in the poorer countries.

The idea behind the tithing concept in Habitat for Humanity is fourfold. First, we acknowledge that God's love knows no national boundaries: "For God so loved the world that he gave . . ." (John 3:16). Second, we know that poverty anywhere in the United States or other developed countries is surrounded by wealth, while poverty in the poorer countries is surrounded by more poverty. Simply put, developing nations need more help from the outside. Third, ten percent of the cost of a typical Habitat house in the United States, Canada, or other developed country will build a complete house—or even more—in a country like India, Uganda, Nicaragua, Peru, or other such developing nation. Finally, it is just good common sense, in addition to being sound religion, to help people where they are so they will not feel compelled to migrate to the U.S. or another wealthy country to have a better life.

Some people object to sending any money overseas. "We have too many problems in our own country. Why are we sending money to those people when it is needed right here?" Although a certain logic supports such thinking, it does not line up with the new way of thinking that is called for by Jesus, nor is it the new thinking that will bring peace on earth and goodwill to all people.

In numerous places in the Bible, the urgent message is delivered that a new way of thinking is called for to be pleasing and acceptable to God. One such scripture is in the book of Romans:

> Therefore I urge you, brothers, in view of God's mercy, to offer your bodies as living sacrifices, holy and pleasing to God—this is your spiritual act of worship. Do not conform any longer to the pattern of this world, but be

transformed by the renewing of your mind. Then you will be able to test and approve what God's will is—his good, pleasing, and perfect will. (12:1-2)

Another clear message in reference to a new way of thinking or a "new self" is found in Ephesians:

You were taught, with regard to your former way of life, to put off your old self, which is being corrupted by its deceitful desires; to be made new in the attitude of your minds, and to put on the new self, created to be like God in true righteousness and holiness. (4:22-24)

One person who has certainly put on a "new self" is former President Jimmy Carter. (Actually, his "new self" is more in relation to other former presidents than to himself. He has been a lifetime practicing Christian who was ridiculed by some during his campaign for the presidency for being a "born-again" person.) Since leaving the White House, President Carter has immersed himself in a host of activities, almost all of which have been for the cause of world peace and helping the poor of the world. He and his wife, Rosalynn, repeatedly traverse the globe to encourage reconciliation between warring groups, to promote the elimination of disease, to foster better farming methods, and to aid and assist several other good causes. Many commentators have remarked that Jimmy Carter has set a new and tremendously high standard for ex-presidents. His whole manner of life carries the hallmark of servanthood.

President Carter became an active participant in Habitat for Humanity in 1984 following my invitation extended to him and Rosalynn at their home in Plains, Georgia, early that year. The full story of how they became involved is in my book, *No More Shacks!*[6]

His first highly publicized involvement came in the autumn of 1984 when he led a group of volunteers from our headquarters in Americus to New York City to help renovate a six-story building for nineteen needy families. He rode on the bus with the other volunteers. (Rosalynn flew up; both returned to Georgia on the bus at the end of the work week.) We traveled all night, arriving in New York on a Sunday afternoon. The Carters, asking for no special favors, stayed in an inner-city church with all the other volunteers. President Carter bunked with the men; Rosalynn had a bunk bed in quarters with the women. The pastor offered the Carters a private bedroom, the only one in the church, but they declined, giving it instead to a newlywed couple in our group.

Every year since, the Carters have spent at least a full week working on Habitat projects. Each time they have stayed with the volunteers. In Tijuana, Mexico, in 1990, when the volunteers were housed in tents, the Carters slept in a tent, also. When it comes to work, they outdo everybody. At the blitz-building in Atlanta in 1988, President Carter was putting down flooring at one o'clock in the morning while everyone else was asleep!

During the Christmas holidays of 1991, President Carter and Rosalynn worked three full days, helping build a new house for a needy family in their hometown of Plains. We finished that house after six o'clock on Christmas Eve and then put up a tree for the family to enjoy on the next day.

The Carters have certainly been a blessing, and continue to be a blessing, to the expanding work of Habitat for Humanity. Both President Carter and Rosalynn are good examples of "born-again" or "re-fathered" lives. They inspire all who know and are privileged to work with them.

Furthermore, President Carter constantly encourages the cooperation and working together of different groups, especially all the churches and synagogues, to accomplish what God has given us to do. He is an ardent advocate of "the theology of the hammer" and all that such a theology implies.

Julio Barrios, national coordinator of Habitat for Humanity in Guatemala, is not as well known a Habitat partner as the former president of the United States, but he spoke just as eloquently at a house dedication service about the vision and "good news" of Habitat and of the beautiful partnerships of the work in that Central American nation:

> The rich have their parties to show off their new houses, to impress their neighbors with how much money they have spent; they invite the architect or builder, who charges an exorbitant fee because he is famous, and is eager to make more money with each house he builds. But the poor have their party and invite their neighbors to see what a good house they have for such a cheap price, and to tell them that they too can have the same, with hard work and sharing. They invite the mason, the only paid laborer, who has charged these families less than the going rate because he believes also in the vision of Habitat and that working together to reduce costs, they can provide even more houses for their neighbors.
>
> The former party is the "old news"; the latter is the "good news." The gospel is the "good news," that we can work together with love for each other—not only for ourselves—and that Catholic and Protestant can work together to bring about the kingdom, because God is righteous and will not forget his people.

"The theology of the hammer" calls for changing the assumptions about poverty and poor people. Poverty housing can actually be eliminated in Americus and in Atlanta, Memphis, Houston, Los Angeles, Cleveland, New York, Boston, Miami, Chicago, Kansas City (both of them!), and in all the towns and cities between. Furthermore, the problem of poverty housing and homelessness can be successfully dealt with in Canada, Mexico, India, Africa, Central and South America, Asia, and the rest of the world.

The new way of thinking dictates that we *act* on our concern, doing what we can, believing that small acts of faith and love are blessed and multiplied by God. It calls for talented people not to sign up mindlessly for the highest salary, but to work in those arenas where they are most needed, regardless of compensation.

Churches and other non-profit organizations should be more concerned with the service they render than they are with the size of the salary for their leaders or the magnitude of the pension plan. Some salaries paid today by Christian churches and Christian organizations are unconscionable, and the compensation paid to many leaders in the non-profit and for-profit world in general is even worse. The new way of thinking that lines up with kingdom values calls for restraint. Just because a talented person can command a huge salary does not give that person a divine right to do so! Servanthood is mandated by new-order living. That kind of life begins to change the world and usher in the heavenly kingdom.

A man who has long been an inspiration to me is Hugh O'Brien from Baillieborough, Ireland. Now in his seventies, Hugh has volunteered with Habitat for Humanity off and on since 1983. He walked with Linda and me from Americus to Indianapolis that year and joined us again in 1986 and 1988 for marathon walks from Americus to Kansas City and from Portland, Maine, to Atlanta. For over forty years, he has been a roving volunteer, doing good works for many charitable organizations all over the world. A humble and gentle man, he lives very simply. He once said to me, "I would never waste my time working for money!"

Think about that. The statement is profound. How many people do precisely what Hugh O'Brien says he would never do? My good friend Tony Campolo—the well-known evangelist, author, and former Habitat for Humanity International board member—once told me about a man who accompanied him to Haiti to work in an extremely poor community. After a couple of weeks, when it was time to return home, the man was visibly sad. Tony asked why he was so downcast. He replied that the work there was the most meaningful he had ever done in his life. He was depressed because he had to return to a job he hated.

"Why don't you just stay here then and do what is so meaningful to you?" Tony inquired.

The man was shocked by the question. "I can't," he replied. "This job wouldn't pay much. I've got to go back to the job that will pay enough to cover car payments, house payments, and my other debts. I would love with all my heart to do this work, but I can't afford to."

A few years ago, a bright young man became very interested in Habitat for Humanity. He was seriously considering working in our headquarters in Americus. When he came for an interview, I offered him a job at a reasonable salary—one on which he could have lived very comfortably. All of his needs would have been adequately met. He could even have saved some money. But a big industry offered him triple what we offered. He had a masters degree from Harvard Business School. Common sense and logic in our materialistic society dictated that he go for the money. He did, and for several years he wrote me on a regular basis, telling me about all the things he was acquiring and about how miserable he was in that company.

The new way of thinking dictates that a person go where his or her heart leads, rather than mindlessly chasing dollar signs and meaningless work. If more people would do that, there would be no leadership shortage in organizations like Habitat for Humanity; and we would be further along in solving some of the world's greatest problems such as massive poverty housing and homelessness, starvation, ozone depletion, reforestation, and violent clashes around the world.

My young friend, incidentally, eventually left the company and entered seminary. God would not let him go!

Now, I am not saying that everyone has to quit his or her job and go to work for Habitat for Humanity or enter the ministry. I am saying that a wise person who desires to please God should listen very carefully to that still small voice and respond to it as the spirit dictates. For some, that will involve staying right where they are, but starting to live by kingdom values and principles. It may mean a change of lifestyle that will possibly precipitate some discomfort and ridicule. But, God's new way of thinking calls for it.

If Habitat for Humanity is your cause—if you believe this is God's work and that struggling to build modest but good and solid houses and selling them on a non-discriminatory basis to needy families at no profit and no interest—is a worthy use of your time, talents, and money, then throw yourself into the work with a fervor and enthusiasm that will shock even your closest friends and co-workers.

Think big dreams. Accept the challenge of eliminating poverty housing and homelessness in your town or city. Decide that you will not accept situations in which people who are created in the image of God are living like animals. Determine to do what is necessary to change things. Help set a goal to get everyone into a good house by a certain date. Move on faith. God will move with you; that is a certainty. Publish the vision of a town with no poverty housing as dramatically as you know how, remembering that a vision boldly stated cannot be ignored.

The new, transformed way of thinking calls for action. Reflection and prayer are good and necessary, but action produces changes. Consider the challenging assertions of the book of James:

> What good is it, my brothers, if a man claims to have faith but has no deeds? Can such faith save him? Suppose a brother or sister is without clothes and daily food. If one of you says to him, "Go, I wish you well; keep warm and well fed," but does nothing about his physical needs, what good is it? In the same way, faith by itself, if it is not accompanied by action, is dead. (2:14-17)

A new way of thinking that calls for bold action, and a mindset that is buttressed by prayer and meditation and fortified by creative partnerships, produces results.

What are you waiting for? Ask God to help you change your whole way of thinking and then get moving. God's new order of the spirit is challenging and confronting you. Right now!

Notes

[1]Letter from Albert Einstein to *The New York Times*, 12 June 1953.

[2]For an in-depth study of this subject, see *The Substance of Faith and Other Sermons by Clarence Jordan*, ed. Dallas Lee (New York: Association Press, 1972) 94-97.

[3]Ibid., 21.

[4]You will read more about partnership with churches in the next chapter and about the full scope of the new church relations department in chapter 6.

[5]Tithing was expanded in October 1993 by action of the Habitat for Humanity International Board of Directors to include all Habitat affiliates in the world. In other words, all local Habitat groups in developed and developing countries since that date have been expected to tithe to help other work in developing countries.

[6]Millard Fuller, "A Presidential Partner," in *No More Shacks!* (Waco TX: Word Books, 1986).

President Jimmy Carter's commitment to Habitat for Humanity's mission has been pivotal to its growth worldwide since he and former First Lady Rosalynn Carter joined the effort in 1984. Here President Carter prepares siding during the 1993 Jimmy Carter Work Project in Winnipeg, Manitoba, Canada.
(Photo by Julie Lopez)

President and Mrs. Carter put in long hours and lots of sweat at Habitat building projects. They make an excellent construction team that inspires others in Habitat's work.

Chapter 5

Churches—
Making the Connection

Churches are the primary partners that work with Habitat in an almost infinite variety of creative overlapping circles. We cherish these partnerships with churches because, as I stated in chapter four, I have always seen Habitat for Humanity as a servant of the church and as a vehicle through which the church and its people can express their love, faith, and servanthood to needy people in a very tangible and concrete (literally!) way.

In this chapter we will explore some of the wonderful partnerships Habitat for Humanity has with various churches and church groups. You will learn of some of the many transforming experiences people have had by participating in one or more of these cooperative ventures.

The simplest and most common form of partnership with churches is one in which a local congregation contributes money and recruits volunteers to help build or renovate one or more Habitat houses. Quite often, a church will adopt or sponsor an entire house, furnishing all the money for that house and providing all the volunteers.

The first Adopt-A-House church partner with Habitat for Humanity of Dane County, Wisconsin, was Luther Memorial Church. That congregation raised $25,000 to cover the cost of the building materials, and, during the summer and fall of 1993, volunteers from the church built the house for the DeCordial family.

The Reverend Harvey Peters, pastor of Luther Memorial, said that his church studied several worthwhile organizations in Madison before deciding to support Habitat. One of the deciding factors in the choice was the fact that Habitat works in such a good way with the people served by the ministry.

Dane County Habitat not only partners with Luther Memorial and other local congregations to build houses in Madison and other communities in the county. The affiliate has also chosen to support Habitat's work in the Yure River Basin in northern Honduras, the same work that is supported by the Habitat affiliate in Americus, Georgia. This tithing partnership enables Luther Memorial and other churches in Dane County to build in Honduras while building right at home.

Some congregations enter directly into partnerships with our overseas work. The most faithful congregation in that category is Plymouth Congregational Church in Plymouth, New Hampshire.

I came to know the people of that fine church when I visited in Plymouth and spoke at the church a couple of times back in the late 1960s and early 1970s, prior to our family's going to Africa in 1973 to work in Zaire.

When we started building houses in Zaire in early 1974, I wrote to the people of Plymouth Church and asked them to help. They responded immediately with funds for a house ($2,000), and the church has donated money for a house in Zaire every year since! Also, when a statewide Habitat group was formed in New Hampshire, the church became a contributor with both funds and volunteers. When a local Habitat affiliate was formed in Plymouth in 1983, Plymouth Congregational Church was again among the strong partner churches.

Actually hundreds of other congregations have been supportive of Habitat's international work, either directly through Habitat for Humanity International or through the tithing program of a local Habitat affiliate. (Over the years, through the effective use of appropriate technology, we have been able to reduce the cost of many houses in developing countries to as little as $700.)

Many congregations have developed a special partnership with Habitat for Humanity International headquarters in Americus. Perhaps the most long-lasting and fruitful of those partnerships has been with Bethel United Church of Christ in Freelandville, Indiana. The happy relationship with those good people in southern Indiana dates back to October 1982, when I spoke at the annual Mission Festival service at the church.

Six months later, Oscar and Lydia Berger, dedicated members of that church, visited us in Americus and toured the Habitat offices and house-building projects on their return trip home from a Florida vacation. When they arrived back in Freelandville, Oscar challenged a couple of the adult Sunday School classes at church to go to Americus the next winter to help build Habitat houses. In February 1984, twenty men came and worked for two weeks. Every year since, a group of men and women from that church have come to Americus to help build houses for needy families and also to help build a new office complex and child care center. They have brought generous contributions, too! Furthermore, as the word spread about these annual trips, people in other churches began to come with the Bethel contingent.

The experiences of the Bethel folks in Americus made them more conscious of needs in their own home area. As a result, Knox County Habitat for Humanity was organized in 1990, the twenty-first Habitat affiliate in Indiana. Bethel Church, along with a United Methodist church and another United Church of Christ, spearheaded the formation of this new Habitat affiliate. A year later, the new group dedicated its first house.

Another church with a very special and long-lasting partnership with Habitat for Humanity International in Americus is Saxonburg Memorial Presbyterian Church in Saxonburg, Pennsylvania. For more than a decade, Jim and Bonnie Gordon, outstanding youth leaders of that congregation, have brought their youth group to Americus every year, and sometimes twice a year, for work camps. In recent years, they have also gone to Habitat work camps in Nicaragua and Florida. Furthermore, their experiences with Habitat in Americus and elsewhere resulted in the formation of a Habitat affiliate in their local area, Habitat for Humanity of Butler County, founded in 1989.

As I travel across the country and around the world visiting Habitat projects, I have observed that the strongest ones are those with the closest ties and strongest connections with the local religious community. I think that is true because such relationships fortify the Christian witness of Habitat and provide the spiritual strength to bridge the rough spots that all Habitat affiliates experience from time to time.

Churches provide reliable, sustained support, whereas many other groups give support for a while and then move on to support something else, or nothing else! Someone once said that vague feelings of humanitarianism will not sustain long-term action. Churches, responding out of love for God, provide the support for long-term action.

Atlanta Habitat for Humanity, one of the largest and most successful affiliates in the United States, enjoys the support of more than a hundred congregations of many denominations. As a consequence, Atlanta Habitat has a steady stream of funds and volunteers that has enabled it to increase the number of houses it builds every year. By 1993, the affiliate was building nearly forty houses a year, and that number is expected to increase to 100 houses a year by 1996, the year the Olympic games come to Atlanta. That year, Atlanta Habitat also plans to fund the building of 100 more houses in its sister project in Mexico City. (Much additional support is given for the work in Atlanta by numerous businesses and other organizations, including community foundations, and hundreds of individuals, but the generous church support is the strong centerpiece of the overall support system.)

The most generous church that supports Atlanta Habitat is Peachtree Presbyterian Church, which is pastored by Dr. Frank Harrington. This dynamic congregation of over 10,000 members (the largest Presbyterian church in the United States) made a five year commitment to Atlanta Habitat in 1989, to give $100,000 a year and 1,000 volunteers to help revitalize the Reynoldstown neighborhood in south Atlanta. The partnership was such a good experience for both sides that it was renewed in

1993. The Peachtree commitment is, incidentally, the largest of any single congregation in the world! The entire Habitat for Humanity organization is enormously grateful to the church and to Dr. Harrington.

The most famous church that supports Atlanta Habitat for Humanity is Ebenezer Baptist, pastored by Dr. Joseph Roberts. For many years, this downtown church was served by Dr. Martin Luther King, Sr., as senior pastor and, for several years prior to his assassination, by Dr. Martin Luther King, Jr., associate pastor. I had the privilege of preaching at Ebenezer in December 1993. The church subsequently committed to sponsor a Habitat house in Atlanta in 1994. The appreciation for the blossoming partnership with this historic congregation is tremendous.

Just to the north of Atlanta, in Cobb County, is another dynamic Habitat affiliate with very strong church partnerships. That group, founded by our good friend Chrys Street in 1986, had completed twenty-six houses by the end of 1993. Of those, fifteen were sponsored by churches.

Linda and I visited Cobb County Habitat on Sunday, September 5, 1993. I spoke at the morning service of St. James Episcopal Church, and in the afternoon we dedicated land for an eighty-three-house Habitat subdivision in the small town of Powder Springs, near Marietta. First Presbyterian Church of Marietta had already blitz-built the first house, which was complete and occupied. A group of four United Methodist churches sponsored another house that was almost completed, and St. James Church sponsored a third that was also nearly finished. Nearby, five Catholic churches had joined together to renovate four more houses that, at the time of our visit, were close to completion. Since our visit, Mt. Bethel United Methodist Church has built two Habitat houses and is committed to building one house every year.

Another fine group with plans for a major subdivision is Valley of the Sun Habitat for Humanity of Phoenix, Arizona. Debi Bisgrove, president of the affiliate, and her husband, Jerry, were instrumental in acquiring land in 1993 for a 200-house Habitat development in the city. Debi expects churches in the area to be a major source of funding for the project, which should be completed within the next six years.

Evansville, Indiana Habitat for Humanity is yet another affiliate with an enviable record of success and with very strong church support. Inspired by Jim Perigo, dedicated Habitat partner and prominent masonry contractor in town, Evansville Habitat built twenty-one houses in a week in 1992. Thirteen of the houses were sponsored by churches. The twenty-first house, as reported earlier, was designated as the 15,000th house built worldwide by Habitat for Humanity. By early 1994, Evansville Habitat had built sixty-five houses. In 1995, they plan to build twenty-five houses in a week in an ambitious project they are calling "25 in '95." Be assured they will do it, and that most of the houses will be sponsored by their partner churches.

In neighboring Illinois, in the little town of Gridley, exciting things have been happening that represent a classic example of one very important aspect of "the theology of the hammer," namely bringing a diverse group of churches together to build a Habitat house. Gridley is a thirty-minute ride north of Bloomington, Illinois, site of the headquarters of McLean County Habitat for Humanity. In August 1991, ground was broken for a house to be built in Gridley. Individuals from the various churches had worked together on community projects in Gridley, but as churches, there had been little cooperation. Habitat changed that. Over the next several months, United Methodists, Roman Catholics, Lutherans, Christians (Disciples of Christ), Apostolic Christians, and Mennonites worked together to get the job done. At the house blessing, when all the work was finished, the community gathered to celebrate what God had done for the Collins family and for the whole community. Pastors and lay people from all the churches worshiped and sang together. The theme song for McLean County Habitat is "Bless Be the Tie That Binds." How very appropriate in Gridley!

Still another incredibly successful Habitat project with a backbone of strong church support is the Charlotte, North Carolina, affiliate. When the Jimmy Carter work camp was held there in 1987 to blitz-build fourteen houses in a week, a total of eighty-six churches signed on to give support in one way or another.

Over the next six years, Charlotte Habitat, under the capable leadership of Susan Hancock, built or renovated over 150 houses. Currently, more than a hundred diverse congregations support that work. As with Atlanta Habitat, Charlotte also enjoys widespread support from all segments of the community, but the strong church support has been, and continues to be, so essential to its phenomenal success.

(Because of her outstanding work in Charlotte, in April 1993, Susan was appointed by Habitat for Humanity International as director of all Habitat work in the United States. Bert Green was named to succeed Susan in Charlotte. Under his excellent leadership, the work is continuing at a very rapid pace.)

In October 1993, Charlotte Habitat blitz-built twenty-two houses in a week. Fourteen of them were partially or totally sponsored by churches. Linda and I had the privilege of being present for the dedication of those houses. The twenty-two-house blitz-build, incidentally, was the kickoff for a ten-month series of over a hundred special events throughout the nation and around the world planned as a part of the "Road to L. A.," leading to the eighteenth-anniversary celebration of Habitat for Humanity at Loyola Marymount University in the Los Angeles area August 4-6, 1994.

Just two months after dedicating the twenty-two houses, Linda and I were back in Charlotte to help blitz-build the 25,000th Habitat house in the world. Volunteers from many churches raised the walls and put on the roof for that historic house. Late in the afternoon, with the sun setting and the temperature falling, I was helping nail the shingles to the roof. The temperature was so cold I could not feel the nails when I would reach into my nail apron for them! That milestone observance was another of the special events on the "Road to L. A." Early in 1994, Charlotte passed another milestone when the affiliate built its 200th house, the first Habitat project in the country to reach that exalted number. Charlotte Habitat expects to double that figure by 1998.

One interesting aspect of the church connection in Charlotte is how the affiliate works with many congregations. Habitat trains crews to do a certain part of the construction. It may train the people from Friendship Baptist to be a foundation crew, the folks from Covenant Presbyterian to be a dry-wall crew, and members of St. Gabriel Catholic Church to be a roofing crew. When a house gets to a certain stage of construction, the appropriate church is called to perform the task or tasks its workers have been trained to do.

Yakima Valley Habitat Partners in the state of Washington developed another successful program to involve churches of all sizes and means. There they assess the cost for each section of a Habitat house. Different churches provide volunteers and/or funds for that part of the construction. For example, Central Lutheran donated siding and did painting and inside trim, First Baptist did the fencing, and East Valley Reformed signed on for the electrical work for a house that was built recently.

In eastern Washington, Spokane Habitat for Humanity enjoys strong church support. Linda and I were privileged to be a part of the dedication of that affiliate's nineteenth house in late August 1993. It was built by a consortium of six churches—one Baptist, two Presbyterian, and three United Methodist churches. In all, Spokane Habitat has thirty churches supporting their work with funding and volunteers. This project built five houses in 1993 and expects to build twice that many in 1994, with at least three of them sponsored by churches.

In the Southeast, "Habijax," in Jacksonville, Florida, is another fantastic Habitat project that has strong church support and just keeps eclipsing one success with another. With outstanding leaders like Dick Weber (who became Habitat's Southeast Regional director in February 1994) and Frank Barker, this outstanding group is a true inspiration to all who have learned about its work. It receives assistance of one kind or another from fifty local congregations. Habijax has done several blitzes, including one in June 1993, when seventeen houses were built in five days. Twelve of them were sponsored by churches. The group plans to build its 100th house by June 1994, and the 200th house by December 1996!

Up the coast from Jacksonville is a smaller but equally dynamic affiliate headquartered in Brunswick, Georgia. Ben Slade, president of Habitat for Humanity of Glynn County, reported to me, at a breakfast meeting in December 1993, that church support was the secret of its success. The affiliate has secured sponsorships from Baptist, Presbyterian, Episcopal, and United Methodist congregations and support in various ways from other denominations to build fourteen houses by the end of 1993. "In 1994," Ben said, "we plan to build fourteen more houses and we expect at least eight of them to be sponsored by churches."

Farther up the east coast, Sandtown Habitat for Humanity in Baltimore, Maryland, has an ambitious goal of rehabilitating a hundred row houses in its project area by 1996, with churches sponsoring at least half of them. As of the end of 1993, Sandtown had already achieved that goal, with commitments from fifty churches. Sandtown Habitat's outstanding director, Allan Tibbels, said that thirty-five row houses were completed in 1993, and that work is proceeding at a pace of thirty or more row houses per year.

The Paterson, New Jersey Habitat for Humanity affiliate has been a prime example of the impact of church involvement and support since 1982, when three Christian Reformed Church pastors returning from a conference in Chicago knelt to pray. Their prayer was that the Lord would help them find a way to address the poverty housing problem in the Paterson area. They repeated those prayer sessions in coming months and wrote a proposal to begin a Christ-centered housing ministry.

"The Lord kept directing us to Habitat," recalled John Algera, pastor of the Madison Avenue Christian Reformed Church and one of the original three pastors. He became a key leader with the Paterson affiliate after it was formed in 1984. Many churches joined the effort in coming years. John Algera estimates that well over seventy-five churches—representing a wide range of denominations and sizes—have been involved in the affiliate's work. This partnership has empowered Habitat to make great strides in addressing housing needs in the area. By early 1994, over forty Habitat houses had been built.

In the heartland of America, church support of Habitat is strong. In Lincoln, Nebraska, ten congregations have signed a covenant with Lincoln Habitat for Humanity, and twenty-five more regularly contribute to the work. During Houseraising Week in 1992, the Lutheran Brotherhood teamed up with Lincoln Lutheran Metro Parish and the Evangelical Lutheran Church in America, Nebraska Synod, to blitz-build a house. In 1993, an article was published in the local newspaper about the extensive church support of Habitat for Humanity in Lincoln. Churches there certainly are making a difference!

Churches in Canada are also making a difference. Their support helped make the Jimmy Carter blitz-building in Canada in July 1993 a huge success. In Winnipeg, Manitoba, eighteen houses were blitz-built in five days. Two of them were entirely sponsored by churches or church-related organizations, and churches helped in many other ways with the overall project. The Carters spent most of the week in Winnipeg, working on those eighteen houses, but they did spend Tuesday in Kitchener, Ontario, helping the affiliate there blitz-build ten more houses. Twenty-six Mennonite churches teamed with twelve Catholic churches to sponsor one of the houses. Ten Presbyterian churches and thirteen Lutheran churches sponsored a second house.

All across Canada, Habitat is on the move under the excellent leadership of its national president, Wilmer Martin. By early 1994, Canada had twenty-one Habitat affiliates (scattered among six provinces), and new projects were in the process of formation in more than forty other locations. Everywhere, churches and church partnership are a vital part of the support system, putting "the theology of the hammer" to work. The same is true in Jamaica, the Caribbean nation that is the sister project supported by tithes from the work in Canada.

On the other side of the world, in Australia, Taree Habitat for Humanity in New South Wales also has extensive church support. Although it is a very new Habitat project, thirty-three churches have already promised either financial support or volunteers or both. This support should insure a good success for that new affiliate, one of nine in that country.

A most encouraging and positive implementation of "the theology of the hammer" occurred in the summer and fall of 1993, when a group of twenty Catholics and Protestants from the Republic of Ireland and Northern Ireland came to the United States to work for twelve weeks at Habitat building sites in Georgia, Florida, and Maryland.

Habitat is being organized in Belfast and Derry in Northern Ireland (and also in England). We expect that the volunteer workers who came to the States will return to their respective countries, having had a positive experience of Protestants and Catholics living and working together, and form a solid cadre that can help spread and strengthen the work of Habitat in their local areas.

In the South Pacific, Habitat for Humanity has extensive work in the country of Papua New Guinea. One of our dedicated International Partners there, Al Vitiello, wrote to me about an incident that illustrates how Habitat brings church people together.[1]

There I sat, a Roman Catholic, in a Lutheran church (with a dirt floor!) high in the mountains of Papua New Guinea, listening to a beautiful sermon by a Baptist pastor. I thought to myself, "This is the true essence of the ecumenical spirit of Habitat for Humanity. We are not only building houses but we are also building bridges between the diverse Christian faiths and people of this world!"

As you can see, churches and church people all over the world are volunteering, raising money, and providing leadership for Habitat for Humanity to build an ever growing number of houses. Church involvement, however, is not limited to local congregations. Sometimes, entire denominations or agencies of denominations sign on to partner with Habitat for Humanity in various ways.

In October 1989, the Home Mission Board of the Southern Baptist Convention sponsored a Habitat house with Atlanta Habitat for Humanity. About 200 volunteers, including many staff members of the Board, participated in building the house that was erected over a one-week period.

In June 1993, over fifty commissioners and special guests to the General Assembly of the Presbyterian Church U.S.A. came early to the site of the assembly in Orlando, Florida, to help blitz-build four Habitat houses with Habitat for Humanity of Greater Orlando. The pioneering event was hailed as a success by all who participated, even though the houses did not get completely finished during that week. This was the first such event to be conducted in connection with a national gathering of a denomination.

A similar four-house blitz-build was held two months later in Denver in connection with Pope John Paul II's visit in early August as a part of World Youth Day. This blitz, held over a two-week period in partnership with Denver Habitat for Humanity, was called "Habitat Youth Blitz-Build '93." It included the enthusiastic work of 200 community service participants who represented Catholic youth groups from five states. Local Catholic churches and other denominations provided financial and volunteer support as well, along with college and university groups. The effort was a total success.

From the inception of Habitat's ministry in 1976, the United Methodist Committee on Relief (UMCOR) has been supportive. We have been designated as "an Advance Special" within the denomination so that individuals or local congregations can give support especially designated for Habitat.[2] Every year Habitat International receives designated funds from UMCOR for many of our projects around the world. During Holy Week of 1993, UMCOR also sponsored one of the 20/20,000 houses in Americus.[3] Dr. Kenneth Lutgen, General Secretary of the agency, came to

Americus with several of his top staff people from New York to help build the house. Other partnerships with UMCOR are envisioned for the future. We cherish that wonderful relationship so very much!

The largest commitment, or challenge, ever made by a church organization was that of another United Methodist group, the Southeast Jurisdiction of the United Methodist Church. This jurisdiction is a decision-making body that encompasses the nine southeastern states of Alabama, Florida, Georgia, North Carolina, South Carolina, Kentucky, Tennessee, Virginia, and Mississippi. At the quadrennial meeting held in Lake Junaluska, North Carolina, in July 1992, delegates to the jurisdictional conference unanimously passed a resolution introduced by United Methodist layman and Habitat partner *par excellance*, Luther Millsaps of Tupelo, Mississippi. The resolution calls for at least half of the 13,000 congregations within the jurisdiction to build a house with Habitat or a like organization within the coming four years. That means 6,500 houses!

Many churches have accepted the challenge and are building houses all over the place! United Methodist churches in Mississippi, especially, have taken the initiative. Marshall L. Meadors, Jr., resident bishop of the Mississippi Area of the United Methodist Church, has strongly encouraged the 1,260 churches in the state to meet the challenge as soon as possible by building *at least* one Habitat house.

One Mississippi Church that has enthusiastically accepted the challenge is the Wells United Methodist Church in Jackson. That unique congregation of dedicated folks is known in Jackson as one of the churches that "stayed behind." Wells is located in the inner city. As the area began to decline, the church made a conscious decision to stay put.

When the 300-member congregation decided to build a Habitat house, it specifically asked to build somewhere in the community around the church. Metro Jackson Habitat for Humanity worked closely with the church and was able to obtain a lot only half a block away on which was an empty, dilapidated house. Metro Jackson Habitat immediately tore the house down, much to the delight of the neighbors.

A modified blitz schedule was agreed upon so that the house could be built on five Saturdays. The church erected a large sign on the lot that proclaimed, "A Wells Built Home—Wells Church, in service to Jesus Christ and this community, is building a house in partnership with Habitat for Humanity." One man, upon seeing the sign, stopped his car, jumped out and ran over to the site to exclaim, "I'm an electrician and I'll wire your next one free!"

The house was finished on schedule and—encircled by a wide red ribbon with a big bow—dedicated on a crisp but sunny Saturday, December 12, 1992. After this project, six more churches in the greater midtown area immediately began working on Habitat houses. These houses were completed in late 1993. More are planned for 1994 by the Wells Church and five additional congregations. Signs are very good for a significant reversal in the decline of the neighborhood.

Another church that took up the challenge was Suntree United Methodist Church in Melbourne, Florida. The pastor, Jeffrey D. Hoy, wrote a moving account of what the experience meant to the congregation—how they received so bountifully even as they were giving.

> The dream of our church building a Habitat house began with the challenge for United Methodist churches to attempt to build one Habitat house. That challenge sparked the possibility among leaders in our congregation, yet such a large undertaking seemed too difficult at first. The more we dreamed about a Habitat house, the more the excitement seemed to grow. The final decision to commit to an entire house was encouraged when a family in our church donated a lot. We then realized that we could actually undertake the building of a house from "the dirt to the shingles."
>
> It was still a difficult decision for our administrative council. We faced a $5,000 deficit in our church operating budget and a needed building program of our own. Yet, leaders were convinced that God would have us serve others first. It would take a great leap of faith. Once we made that commitment—that step of faith—things began to happen quickly. People began to commit money and time. Plans were pulled together, and we began to raise funds.
>
> "Our Habitat House" began as a dream of giving—and yet we never realized that it would become a dream of receiving. We set out to be a blessing to others—and we had no idea what a blessing this effort would be to our own church. There were many little blessings along the way, but two wonderful things that happened in our congregation stand out.
>
> First, there was a great blessing of fellowship. Our church revived a sense of strong fellowship and pulling together that was reminiscent of our beginnings as a church eight years earlier when we built our first building. New friendships and experiences will forever be a part of our memory.
>
> Secondly, there was a financial blessing. The Bible speaks of sowing and reaping. Somehow, what we receive is related to what we give. This is the teaching of Jesus. The great truth that we learned is that as you give, you will receive. We began our dream with a $5,000 deficit in our church operating budget and ended the year with the entire house paid for and almost completely built and a nearly $10,000 surplus. We were actually able to give nearly $4,000 above the cost of "Our House" to Habitat! The next year, our giving increased nearly sixty percent, and we over pledged our building fund goals by nearly fifty percent.
>
> How can you explain such blessing except to say, "Give and it will be given unto you, pressed down, shaken together and running over"? To the church that might say to itself, "We cannot afford to be in mission, to look beyond ourselves. Our own financial constraints are too great," I would respond, "You cannot afford NOT to be in mission, NOT to look beyond yourself. The seed that is sown in God's mission for God's children will return a hundred-fold to those who plant it."

I feel confident that those ambitious United Methodists in the Southeast jurisdiction will succeed in what they have set out to do. Furthermore, I am sure they will inspire other United Methodist jurisdictions across the land to "go and do likewise." Other denominations will pick up the idea and challenge their local congregations to build Habitat houses.

United Methodists in the Southeast are not the only ones excited about Habitat for Humanity. A truly inspiring story comes from Ohio.

In 1989, the graduating class of the Methodist Theological School in Ohio learned of some students at Ohio Wesleyan University (OWU) in Delaware, Ohio, who were interested in forming a Habitat campus chapter.[4] The class designated its senior class gift as seed money to start the chapter.

At the same time, a student at Methodist Theological School, Randy Lewis, started a three-year internship with Asbury United Methodist Church in Delaware. Because he wanted to work with students at the college anyway, he decided to help organize the Habitat campus chapter.

Randy reported that the students were very enthusiastic about working with Habitat, but that they did not want to drive to Columbus to work. (There was no local Habitat affiliate.) Therefore, they made some contacts with local agencies and offered assistance. Their first task was a simple painting job that built confidence among the students. The next job looked simple, since it only involved putting new roofing on an addition to a house. Completion of that job, however, led to a look inside the house. What they saw was a disaster!

The students went to area churches and requested money and volunteers to help rebuild the whole house. Work days were organized for nearly every Saturday for almost a year until the renovation work was completed. The family lived in the house the entire time the work was underway.

That project provided the impetus for launching a local Habitat affiliate, Delaware County Habitat for Humanity. All the churches that had helped with the extensive renovation work provided the backbone of the new organization, which became official in September 1991. The affiliate's first house was completed, and the family occupied it in March 1992.

Not only did the affiliate organize, but the campus chapter strengthened. During spring break of 1990, Ohio Wesleyan University sent a Habitat work team to work with Columbia, South Carolina Habitat for Humanity. The twenty-two member work team consisted of Christians, Moslems, Buddhists, and a Jewish couple—all putting "the theology of the hammer" to work. In 1991, the spring break trip nearly doubled in size. In 1992, OWU sent two Habitat work teams out, one to Mississippi and one to the Dominican Republic. Also, by that time Delaware County had two International Partners: Erica Holstein in Guatemala and Jim Tull in Nicaragua. In early 1993, students from the campus chapter helped build the second house for the affiliate. Before the year was out, two more houses were completed.

Many Habitat affiliates not only work across denominational lines and with Protestants and Catholics; they also form partnerships across racial and other faith lines.

In Richmond, Virginia, the local Habitat project was the recipient of a house paid for and built by a partnership of Northminster Baptist Church, a white congregation, and Metropolitan African-American Baptist Church. Construction began in October 1993, and the house was finished in March 1994.

In Seminole County, Florida, three very different congregations formed a partnership and built a Habitat house: Love Tabernacle Church of God in Christ, the Congregation of Liberal Judaism, and the Altamonte Community Chapel (United Church of Christ). While differing on a lot of other theology, they all agreed on "the theology of the hammer."

The first partnership between a Christian church and a Jewish synagogue in the Pacific Northwest was forged in 1991, between Holy Trinity Lutheran and Temple B'nai Torah of Seattle, Washington. The two congregations raised all the money needed for a Habitat house to be built in partnership with Seattle Habitat for Humanity. During the summer of 1992, volunteers from the two congregations built it. The house was dedicated in September and the family, a Laotian man and wife and five children, moved in. A house was built as a result of the partnership, but in the process relationships also were built that transcend differences in theology. Sunnie Gordon, dedicated partner with Seattle Habitat for Humanity, had this to say about the pioneering partnership:

> To me, the most exciting thing is not just building a house, but bringing members of a church and a synagogue together . . . to work on a project together. It's "the theology of the hammer"—the symbol of cooperation—at work to solve a problem.

One of the earliest partnerships with a Jewish organization was in 1985 when a group of fifteen volunteers from the American Jewish Society for Service in New York City spent seven weeks helping build three Habitat houses on "Habitat Hill" in Amarillo, Texas. Bolstered by the successful event, Amarillo Habitat encouraged future joint work projects. The experience was so positive that other American Jewish Society of Service work groups have subsequently worked with Habitat projects in St. Louis, Missouri; Chicago, Illinois; and Selma, Alabama.

Flower City Habitat for Humanity in Rochester, New York, one of the really outstanding Habitat affiliates in the United States, is a strong advocate of bringing all sorts of people, organizations, and congregations together to build houses. During their 1993 building-blitz week, over 800 volunteers worked on Habitat houses and community projects at eleven different locations. William Gavett, executive director for volunteers, wrote about the diversity of the group and commented in a very meaningful way about that powerful application of "the theology of the hammer":

> They came from as far away as Germany and as close as the next block over. They ranged from the young to the old, skilled and unskilled, male and female, organization affiliated and loners, students-employed-retirees, twenty different religious affiliations—from every walk of life.
>
> For a few hours, we forgot who we were. We found out something new about ourselves through our participation in a Habitat project.
>
> At a Habitat site, "the theology of the hammer" supersedes all other theologies, philosophies, and other deliberative speculations about the nature of life. Focusing on the building of a house for God's cause leaves no time to entertain theological debate nor to ponder the differences in one's brothers and sisters on the job.

"The theology of the hammer" truly does embrace a wide spectrum of beliefs and people. I recall attending a groundbreaking for a new Habitat house in Riverside, California a few years ago. The early morning affair included a breakfast of tripe soup (intestines of a cow) in a Hispanic church, followed by a short parade to the construction site and a brief program consisting of a couple of songs, a scripture reading, a talk by me, the symbolic breaking of the ground with shovels, and a prayer of dedication. Afterwards, because I had another engagement, I started to walk away. At the edge of the lot, I was accosted by a young man who asked to speak to me.

"I am a secular humanist," he stated, "and I didn't like all of that religious stuff at the groundbreaking. It made me uncomfortable."

"Well," I replied, "what did you expect at a groundbreaking of a house to be built by a Christian organization? This work is inspired by God, and our motivation is a religious one. We express that in songs, meditations, and prayers."

"I know," he continued, "but it all makes me feel uncomfortable. I don't like it."

"You've got a problem," I told him, "and that problem is that you have come to work with a Christian group. But, you are welcome. You are needed, and I hope you'll stay and help."

I asked him to show me his hands. He extended them to me. "They will fit nicely around a shovel. Why don't you go back over there and help out? And, if somebody starts talking about God or Jesus, just put some cotton in your ears, or listen in. You might hear something that would be good for you."

He looked at me for a long moment, glanced at his hands, then turned on his heels, and went to get a shovel.

Betty Michelozzi, Habitat partner with Habitat for Humanity of Santa Cruz, California, tells a similar story. At a week-long work camp, a volunteer questioned her to such an extent about her religious affiliation that Betty thought the woman was trying to persuade her to change churches. Later, at the same work camp, another participant came up and exclaimed, "Your devotion this morning was good! I'm an atheist."

"The theology of the hammer" has a broad range, all the way from conservative Christian to liberal Jew, to a secular humanist, to an atheist! All of these incredible partnerships are so very strengthening to this ministry, but the power, the spiritual strength, and the dynamism for this work come primarily from the churches.

Notes

[1]International Partners are people who are trained in Americus at the international headquarters of Habitat for Humanity and then go out to developing countries to work for a period of time, usually three years, at Habitat project sites.

[2]The Advance Special numbers, for the interest of United Methodists, are: Ministry 982375-4 and Construction 982376-5.

[3]See chapter 1, pages 15, 17, 18.

[4]For more information on Habitat's campus chapters program, see chapter 8, pages 94-96.

A 15-house blitz-build by the Lexington, KY Habitat for Humanity in 1991 featured considerable church partici- pation, as exemplified by this hand-painted sign at the site.

Churches play a prominent role in Habitat's inner-city affiliates, among them the ambitious commitment of Sandtown HFH in Balti- more, MD, to renovate 100 row houses in a five-year period. The project is on schedule! (Photo by Dennis Meola)

Several churches of different denominations partnered with each other and Habitat to raise houses during the 20/20,000 blitz-build in Americus, GA —as shown here. (Photo by Dennis Meola)

Chapter 6

A Church Relations Department

Thousands of churches have signed on to partner with Habitat for Humanity, either with a local affiliate in the United States, Canada, Australia, New Zealand, the United Kingdom, Poland, or Hungary, or with one or more of the several hundred Habitat projects in developing countries.

Churches of various sizes and means support Habitat for Humanity in a variety of ways.

- Many churches make annual or other regular donations to a specific Habitat affiliate or to Habitat for Humanity International.
- Some congregations agree to donate a certain sum of money to their local affiliate each time a Habitat house is begun or dedicated.
- Others agree to raise the funds and provide the labor for a designated construction task such as roofing or framing.
- Larger churches or several congregations working in partnership can adopt (or sponsor) a Habitat house by raising the funds and providing the labor for construction. All work in this Adopt-A-Home program is conducted under the leadership of the local Habitat affiliate, which may also seek businesses, civic clubs, or individuals to provide financial and labor support to churches.
- A number of churches sign an annual, renewable agreement to become a covenant church. Covenant churches make a pledge to pray for Habitat's ministry, contribute financially, and provide volunteers to build Habitat houses or perform other tasks associated with Habitat's work. Beyond that, each covenant church determines its own commitment.

Habitat for Humanity has had a covenant church program for years. The idea originated in the New England states in the early 1980s as a way to involve local church congregations in the growing ministry of Habitat. In 1987, Habitat for Humanity International board member Warren Sawyer proposed the covenant church idea to the international board, and it was unanimously adopted for the worldwide work of Habitat. The program has grown steadily ever since.

These are some of the typical ways covenant churches help to support Habitat for Humanity:

- Spread the word about Habitat's ministry throughout the community.
- Have members serve on the local Habitat board of directors or on a committee of the board.
- Furnish office space and/or telephone, fax, copier, or office personnel.
- Help collect eyeglasses for "Vision Habitat." (Through this program, used eyeglasses are shipped overseas to be sold at minimal cost. The funds raised are used to build houses. Hence, the program serves the dual purpose of helping people have better vision and building Habitat houses.)[1]
- Conduct an "Extraordinary Gift" Christmas market campaign, offering people the opportunity to "purchase" construction supplies to build houses as an alternative to traditional holiday gift giving. (Information about this program is available from Habitat for Humanity International or from a local Habitat affiliate.)
- Distribute Habitat "house banks" and devotional guides to members.
- Encourage support of the local and worldwide work of Habitat for Humanity by inviting local or international volunteers to speak in the church.
- Participate in the Global Village program by sending one or more members of the church to a work camp in a developing country.[2]
- Observe the International Day of Prayer and Action for Human Habitat annually on the third Sunday of September. This special observance is a way that all churches—not only those who have made a covenant with Habitat—can join together on a particular day to help make shelter a matter of conscience throughout the nation and around the world. Songs, prayers, litanies, responsive readings, and even sermons are directed toward raising awareness of the problems of poverty housing and homelessness and are designed to provoke persons to action.

The growing involvement of churches and church organizations in Habitat's ministry prompted the realization that we needed a separate department to coordinate this work and to expand it as rapidly as possible. When conversations first began about forming the church relations department late in 1992, Jeff Snider, our then executive vice president of Habitat for Humanity International, approached Rick Beech about accepting the job as director. Rick would not only be director of the department—he would create it. Rick accepted the offer immediately and began setting up the new office in Murfreesboro, Tennessee, near Nashville, where he was living.

Rick was eminently qualified for the task by education, experience, and interest. He holds a master of divinity degree from Southeastern Baptist Theological Seminary in Wake Forest, North Carolina. While working in a local church through an internship in 1984, Rick and others in the congregation and throughout the community became excited about starting a housing ministry. Their efforts led to the formation of the Wake County Habitat affiliate. Rick served as part-time coordinator of the affiliate until he graduated from the seminary, at which time he became Wake County Habitat's executive director. Wake County Habitat became one of the strongest Habitat projects in the nation. Rick was especially successful in forging many partnerships with local churches. He loudly proclaimed that churches were the backbone of Habitat's work.

After Rick left the Wake County affiliate to direct the work of affiliates in Kentucky and Tennessee, he continued to seek church support. He signed me up to be the speaker for Revival '92, a week-long series of services across the two states held during September 1992. Worship services, held in a different location each day, were tied in with construction of more than fifty Habitat houses. Ground was broken on some houses, while work was begun or continued on others. Many houses were blitz-built during Revival '92 week, and several announcements were made about house construction that would soon begin. Although many other organizations and individuals contributed to the success of Revival '92, the concentrated effort to enlist churches to sponsor homes or to help in whatever way they could made revival week a great witness to the power of God's love in Tennessee and Kentucky.

Actually, the idea for a week of blitz-building came from Alan Riggs, a super Habitat partner from Kingsport, Tennessee. I had met Alan and his wife, Debbie, when I led a spiritual renewal weekend at Colonial Heights Presbyterian Church in his hometown in the summer of 1988.

The story behind our meeting is quite remarkable. Alan and Debbie are not members of Colonial Heights Presbyterian. (They are Southern Baptists.) The week before I arrived in town to lead the renewal weekend, Alan was home one evening reading the current issue (June) of *Reader's Digest*. In that issue was an article about Habitat for Humanity and me, entitled "Millard Fuller's Blueprint for Success."

As Alan was reading that article, Debbie was reading the local paper. When Alan finished the *Reader's Digest* article, he turned to Debbie and started telling her about it. He concluded by remarking, "I'd sure like to meet that Millard Fuller."

"Well," Debbie responded, "you won't have to wait long. He's coming to Kingsport this weekend to speak at Colonial Heights Presbyterian Church. There's an article about him and his forthcoming visit here in tonight's paper."

Alan was amazed. He and Debbie contacted the church and made arrangements to attend the weekend gathering. I got to know Alan there and learned that he and Debbie were dedicated Christians, and that Alan was a skilled builder with his own construction company. I immediately invited him to be a house leader at the Jimmy Carter blitz-building project that was to be held a few weeks later in Atlanta. Alan accepted the invitation. He felt strongly that God had brought us together.

In Atlanta, Alan did a great job as a house leader. He became thoroughly infected with "habititis," learned more about "the theology of the hammer," and gained a lot of practical knowledge about how to do blitz-building. When he returned from the Carter project, Alan called the pastor of Colonial Heights Church, David Wadsworth, and offered to supervise a blitz-built house for the local Habitat affiliate, Holston Habitat for Humanity, if the church would raise the money and provide the volunteer workers.

David had wanted to do this very thing, so he viewed Alan's call as providential. Already a few members of the church had felt led to build a Habitat house, but approval was needed from the whole congregation. Only if everybody supported the project would it have a chance to succeed. At least a hundred volunteers and $25,000 to purchase the building materials would be needed.

David had long had the vision of his church's doing a blitz. He had been one of the original board members of Holston Habitat, but he had doubts and questions: "How can a church that regularly struggles to raise its own budget and find enough volunteers to conduct its normal programs possibly undertake such a large project as building a Habitat house?" Still, the thought persisted that God wanted the church to take this leap of faith. David prayed to be shown the way for his blitz-building hopes to be translated into reality.

Alan's phone call was the beginning of David's prayer being answered. The seemingly outrageous goal of building a house in five days captured the imaginations of the people in the church. At a congregational meeting following worship one Sunday in late August 1988, a specific proposal was approved to build a five-day blitz house in late October.

In the weeks following, David said, "The money and the volunteers turned up like quails and manna in the Sinai wilderness!" All the money was raised, and the house was built and finished on schedule.

David wrote an article about this blitz house. "The Church and the Five-Day Miracle" was the feature article in the November 1989 issue of the *Presbyterian Survey*, the national magazine of the Presbyterian Church U.S.A. In that article, he pointed out what wonderful things had happened in his congregation as a result of the project. He also told of the ripple effect with other churches, inspiring both local congregations and others in distant cities to undertake similar projects. He concluded the article by reporting that Colonial Heights wanted to do it again! David and Alan also wrote an excellent step-by-step manual entitled *Your Church Can Be a Blitz-Builder Too!* that guides churches in organizing a Habitat blitz-built house. Colonial Heights Church and David Wadsworth have continued to be vitally involved with Holston Habitat for Humanity. Colonial Heights built its fourth Habitat house during Holy Week 1994.

Following the construction of the blitz house in 1988, Alan continued his active involvement, including the supervision of other Habitat houses for Holston Habitat over the next few years. That work was not enough for him, however. Wanting to do more, he wrote to me asking for a bigger challenge. I put him in touch with Rick Beech to find out how he could help throughout Tennessee and Kentucky.

Rick and Alan became fast friends. Alan proposed that blitz-building be done across the two states during a particular week. Rick added the theme of revival. The result was Revival '92. Linda and I agreed to join the effort, and, as related earlier, I signed on as the revival speaker. Over a six-day period, we would have special revival services in Lexington and Lebanon, Kentucky; and Knoxville, Chattanooga, Memphis, and Nashville, Tennessee.

Plans were carefully laid for the first revival service in Lexington. The Habitat affiliate there is one of the best in the nation. With capable leaders like Lyle Hanna, Sara Coppler (who became director for the region in 1993), Cecil Dunn, Kirk Kirkpatrick, and many others, it has become a truly outstanding project.

The previous year, in the summer of 1991, Lexington Habitat had blitz-built fifteen houses in connection with the fifteenth anniversary blitz-building campaign of Habitat for Humanity International. Linda and I were there on the concluding weekend of that successful event, along with the actor Paul Newman. Eleven churches sponsored homes in that project, and twenty-four others provided support in various ways.

Lexington Habitat signed on to do an even bigger project in connection with Revival '92. Working with nine Habitat affiliates in surrounding towns, Lexington organized the "Bluegrass 20," named for the twenty houses to be built in central Kentucky during the revival week. By the end of the week, Lexington Habitat had built ten houses, Boyle County Habitat had completed two church-sponsored houses, and the other area affiliates had built one house each. Over forty churches and a Jewish congregation supported the project through the ten-county area.

Before work began, however, the blessings started to flow on Sunday evening during the first revival service at Central Christian Church. Several hundred people attended from Lexington and neighboring cities and towns where blitz-building was getting underway.

I talked about the importance and historical significance of the week. We are redefining revival, I explained. No longer is a revival just a series of worship services where people are spectators and the preacher talks about "Gawd" and "Jeesus." True revival, I said, must extend beyond the walls of the church. After Revival '92 services, you go home to get a bit of rest. Then, you get your hammers and nails and go out to build some needy family a house. That is what true revival is all about—putting faith and love to work!

I pointed out that our coming to church should inspire and motivate us to make a difference in the world. The challenge of the Bible is to let our light so shine in dark places that others can see our good works and glorify our Father who is in heaven. We can blind each other by only shining our lights inside the church. We must take our lights outside. That was being done in and around Lexington during the week, as well as in many other places all across Kentucky and Tennessee.

I also commented on how all the churches were working so harmoniously together to build the houses. The action-oriented, love-in-action, faith-at-work emphasis of the week and the working together of so many different churches and other groups was the very essence and incarnation of true revival and "the theology of the hammer."

Kirk Kirkpatrick, who was then Lexington's executive director, said that the revival experience went far beyond the massive blitz-building program. "Revival '92," he said, "has given us an understanding of Habitat's effect on churches—a realization that building a house in partnership with God's people in need will revive a church and bring God's spirit to the church and to the community."

The second revival service was in Lebanon, sixty miles south of Lexington. The Habitat project there had been started by Pat and Ilona Burdette, who had met a few years earlier when both of them were volunteers at Habitat headquarters in Americus. When they married and moved back to Pat's hometown of Lebanon, they were determined to start a local group. Their good efforts resulted in My New Kentucky Home Habitat for Humanity being officially organized in December 1990. In planning for Revival '92, affiliate leaders put a new twist on blitz-building. Four principal churches were each asked to raise the money and provide volunteers on a particular day to complete a specific part of construction. For example, Lebanon Baptist Church was responsible for framing on the first day. Other congregations were assigned their tasks for different days of the week, and several churches joined together the last day to finish the project.

We visited the site Monday afternoon and held our second Revival '92 service that evening.

On day three we were off to Knoxville, Tennessee, in what came to be known as the revival van. Alan Riggs was usually our driver. (Alan's wife, Debbie, joined the revival team on Wednesday in Chattanooga and spent the remainder of the time with us.)

Over the course of the week, as we traveled together, sharing meals, visiting the numerous work sites, and participating in the various revival services, we developed a wonderful camaraderie with each other. It seems there was almost constant banter and lots of laughter. Our hearts surely were full of joy. One source of a lot of laughs was the red "fireballs" Rick and Alan ate constantly. Whenever conversation would lag, they would start eating the fireballs and immediately things would liven up. They tried to entice me into their fireballs habit, but after trying to eat one, I decided they were too hot for me. Linda did not particularly like them either!

At every stop on our trip, we had numerous interviews with television, radio, and newspaper people, plus we attended breakfasts, luncheons, and other gatherings in addition to the Revival '92 services. Through all these means, we were able to communicate with thousands of people, many of whom learned about Habitat's ministry for the first time. We also encouraged and strengthened hundreds of dedicated Habitat partners along the way and gave them a deeper understanding of "the theology of the hammer" and a new and expanded definition of revival.

We had another great revival service in Knoxville. Over 400 people attended a lively service at the Fifth Avenue Baptist Church. David Wadsworth drove over from Kingsport to share in the service. He played a guitar and sang an incredible song he had written about Habitat for Humanity. Mike Stevens, construction superintendent with Knoxville Habitat, spoke and showed slides about the work camps he had led with Knoxville Habitat's sister project in Nicaragua.

Five churches (along with other community sponsors) funded and built the five houses that were dedicated or constructed during Revival '92 in Knoxville.

Next we traveled to Chattanooga, where we had a great service at the First Baptist Church at Golden Gateway. An exciting announcement was made at the conclusion of the evening. An Episcopal church would enter into partnership with a white Baptist church and a black Baptist church to build a Habitat house. Chattanooga was about to experience a very dramatic example of "the theology of the hammer."

The blitz was in full swing when we arrived at the "Miracle in Memphis," that city's name for the Revival '92 events. A total of six houses were going up, four of which were sponsored or supported by churches. A Jewish congregation, which began its work with Habitat that week, helped out on all six houses. Obviously, Betty Anne Wilson, executive director, was doing a great job of leading that fine project.

The final city on our revival tour was Nashville. Not only did we have a good service there, but I also was invited to address the annual meeting of the National Fraternal Congress, which was being held at that time in the city. This nationwide organization is the umbrella group for the various fraternal insurance societies in the United States such as Woodmen of the World, Knights of Columbus, Lutheran Brotherhood, Aid Association for Lutherans, Mennonite Mutual Aid, National Catholic Life, Sons of Norway, and over ninety other societies. I had been invited to speak at their national convention in Portland, Oregon, in October 1990. At that time, the congress adopted Habitat for Humanity as a national cause. Ever since, the members had faithfully raised several million dollars for Habitat affiliates across the country and had recruited thousands of volunteers. During the summer, NFC volunteers had built two houses for Nashville Habitat for Humanity.

Another interesting thing happened in Nashville. A few executives of a company that I founded with a partner nearly thirty years earlier, Favorite Recipes Press, attended the revival service. (I no longer have ownership in the company that is now headquartered in Nashville.) As a result of that meeting, a decision was made to produce a Habitat cookbook. Linda served as editor, and a year later, in September 1993, the book was published. By year's end, the book, *Partners in the Kitchen: From Our House To Yours*, had sold over 80,000 copies! Profits from the sale of the book go to build more Habitat houses.

By anyone's measuring standard, Revival '92 was a roaring success. When it was all over, Rick summarized what the experience had meant to him:

> The week was more than I anticipated. The series of revival services established that God is the author of this ministry, and the church should be our foundation. By tapping into the church, we feel that we can build many, many more houses than we have been building. Aside from the impact on churches, communities, volunteers, and homeowners, Revival '92 also made a difference in the lives of many folks who have been around Habitat for a long time. The week, for instance, was a very religious experience for me. It brought me closer to God. It made me realize that I do what I do not because Habitat is a good idea, but because Jesus Christ is the Lord and Savior of my life and I want to emulate Him in this world.

Revival '92 continues to have a great impact on the region. From Revival week in 1992 until early 1994, twenty-three new Habitat affiliates were formed in Kentucky and Tennessee. All of the Habitat projects in the two states participated in the building and renovation of almost 200 houses in 1993, a record in Habitat house construction for that region. Hundreds of churches helped make that possible. Furthermore, the spirit of Revival '92 has been spilling over into other areas and is having a positive impact in those places, too.

As this book goes to press, Rick is beginning to concentrate on developing closer relations with denominational headquarters and other church groups and agencies. One such group is the Cooperative Baptist

Fellowship (CBF). Plans have been laid for this growing fellowship of Southern Baptists to partner with Greater Greensboro Habitat for Humanity in North Carolina to build seven Habitat houses in a blitz-build to take place in connection with the annual convention in Greensboro in May 1994 (just as this book is being published).

The CBF national office and local Baptist churches provided funds for two of the houses. Habitat for Humanity International funded one house and local churches of various denominations in Greensboro raised the money for the remaining houses. Volunteers are to come from all the sponsoring churches and from paticipants in the general assembly. It is hoped that the emerging partnership with the CBF will result in the launching of the ministry of Habitat for Humanity in the eastern European nation of Albania.

Our church relations goal is to involve at least half of the churches in each area where we have a Habitat affiliate. As stated earlier, there are over 350,000 churches in the United States and another 30,000 in Canada. If a Habitat group were to be established in every community, and if we could gain the support of half of the churches in each one, imagine how many houses could be built by 190,000 congregations. And that's just in two countries in North America!

Numbers make assessments possible and enable new strategies to encourage churches to join us, but our primary goal is always to eliminate poverty housing. We are seeking to involve all these churches because we want to build more simple, decent houses for God's people in need.

We know that if we are asking churches to give generously to this work, we have to be sensitive to their situation. Wake County Habitat for Humanity in Raleigh, North Carolina, the affiliate that Rick helped start, realized in 1993 that some of its church supporters were beginning to struggle. Land prices increased and the cost of building single-family houses became prohibitive for many churches. Scott Anderson, executive director of Wake County Habitat, said the affiliate realized the need to design a building project just for churches and the imperative of addressing the unique circumstances of congregations.

The design of this project was one step taken to hold down costs. By building a group of townhouses, instead of single-family houses, the affiliate was able to reduce the price by $7,000 per house. The affiliate also sought support from corporate givers and reduced the church sponsorship price to a more reasonable level. Churches responded, and construction of twenty-two townhouses is planned for the weekend of the International Day of Prayer and Action for Human Habitat in September 1994. Scott said that the interdenominational emphasis of the project is bringing renewed vigor to churches. A joint worship service will be held on the final

Friday night "to keep the focus where it needs to be—on the Lord's work," he said.

The future looks bright for the new church relations department. Rick and his folks certainly have a lot of work to do! They are on the job, though—eating a fireball every now and then to speed them up—and steadily spreading "the theology of the hammer" to more and more churches across the land and around the world.

(For information about involving churches in Habitat projects, contact the Church Relations Department, PO Box 1497, Murfreesboro TN 37133-1497. To order any of the resources mentioned in this chapter or to get information about speakers, contact Habitat for Humanity International, 121 Habitat Street, Americus GA 31709-3498.)

Notes

[1]For more information, write to Vision Habitat, Habitat for Humanity International, 121 Habitat Street, Americus GA 31709-3498.

[2]This program, which sends out short-term work teams of six to thirty people to developing countries to help build Habitat houses, is more fully explained in chapter 9, page 117.

Chapter 7

A Theology of Unity

From the very beginning of Habitat for Humanity, it has been my dream that this ministry be a vehicle through which a wide array of churches and church people could work together. And, I have always seen Habitat for Humanity as a servant of the church.

It is a shame that the church of Jesus Christ, which reads the same Bible—albeit in many translations and versions—is so divided. Differing doctrines and conflicting interpretations of scripture have divided Christendom into groupings of an almost infinite number.

Habitat for Humanity, however, has brought many churches together. In the process, partnerships have been formed among people who have never worked cooperatively on anything! Volunteers have discovered that the things that make them the same are more important than their differences in race, economic class, nationality, or theology. People leave behind their differences when they agree on the hammer as an instrument of God's love.

My fervent prayer is that putting "the theology of the hammer" into practice will bring more and more churches together so that our combined lights will be so bright that millions of people will see our good work and God will be glorified as never before. We will make shelter such a matter of conscience that we will, in fact, eliminate poverty housing and homelessness.

Maybe, just maybe, God wants to use "the theology of the hammer" as a means to draw His divergent family closer together. Perhaps God is calling us to issue a joint invitation to "the strangers" of this world to come in and enjoy the abundant life that Jesus said he came to bring.

Can you think of a better idea for drawing the churches together? What better symbol to rally around than a hammer—the tool of Jesus as he worked in the carpenter's shop of Joseph and the tool that was used to nail him to the cross! Churches can increasingly use this simple instrument to show God's love in action by building and renovating houses for families in need. A doubting and sinful world can see that we in the church can agree on something and that God's love is manifest in our work. Every house Habitat builds is a *sermon* about God's love.

The message from the Bible is certainly clear that we should strive constantly for unity and to also work together. Jesus himself prayed that his disciples be one.

As you sent me into the world, I have sent them into the world. For them I sanctify myself, that they too may be truly sanctified. My prayer is not for them alone. I pray also for those who will believe in me through their message, that all of them may be one, Father, just as you are in me and I am in you. May they also be in us so that the world may believe that you have sent me. (John 17:18-21)

Paul encouraged the church of Corinth, to "agree with one another so that there may be no divisions among you and that you may be perfectly united in mind and thought" (1 Cor 1:10).

The church, unfortunately, did not remain united. Division began immediately, with congregations developing their own doctrines and practices and then fighting with one another over who was right. Various councils and churches gathered for centuries to discuss beliefs, develop creeds, and attempt to understand the church worldwide.

Martin Luther nailed his Ninety-five Theses to the church door in Wittenberg, Germany in 1517, and, thus, launched the Protestant Reformation. That event eventually set off bloody fighting between Catholics and Protestants; soon, even the Protestants were killing each other over doctrinal differences.

Division and splintering continued almost unabated until the twentieth century. Early in this century, though, a movement began to encourage cooperation between and among churches. Sunday School workers, missionaries, and others—primarily university students—started meeting together to pray and plan ways they could overcome their differences and work together.

In 1910, following a world conference of missionary societies in Edinburgh, Scotland, the word ecumenism began to signify a concern to reunite the divided Christian family.[1] The purpose of the conference was to develop a missionary strategy that would make a better collaborative use of resources. These ideas of unity and mission came to define the ecumenical movement that was born in Edinburgh. Delegates from that meeting continued to organize and focus on three ideas: missions, common service of the church, and discussion of divisive doctrinal issues.

Supporters of the ecumenical movement realized that unification would not happen immediately and probably not in their lifetimes, so they searched for places where they could find oneness. The Commission on Life and Work was formed to identify areas where divided churches could agree and relate. "Doctrine divides, service unites" became the commission's slogan. More than 600 delegates from thirty-seven countries attended the commission's first conference in Stockholm in 1925 to discuss the role of the church in areas such as international relations, education, economics, and industry.

The World Conference on Faith and Order, which met in Lausanne, Switzerland in 1927, was another attempt for churches to understand one another.

Various other groups met during the 1920s and 1930s to discuss the doctrinal issues that divided the church and to seek unity. At another Edinburgh conference in 1937, unanimous agreement was reached on a statement about "the grace of our Lord Jesus Christ." Differences remained, however, concerning ideas about the church, the sacraments, and ministry. Supporters of ecumenism agreed that their task was not so much to *create* unity, which is a gift of God, but to *exhibit* unity in Christ and not let their differences be the most important issues.

In 1938, church leaders from two ecumenical groups, the Faith and Order Commission and the Commission on Life and Work (which both evolved from the 1910 Edinburgh Conference), agreed to work out proposals for a merger and began plans to form a world council of churches.

The rise of Adolph Hitler and the horrors of the Nazi regime interrupted the plan to unite the churches officially, but sparked the sentiment that "the world is too strong for a divided church." During the war, a small ecumenical group organized refugee relief efforts and instituted communications systems for Christians torn apart by the fighting.

Following World War II, representatives from 147 churches met in Amsterdam in August 1948, and organized the World Council of Churches (WCC). The council defined itself as "composed of churches which acknowledge Jesus Christ as God and Savior." Despite misunderstandings from the beginning, the council did not see itself as a superchurch, but sought to enable churches. Most of the churches initially represented were European or North American. Since then the number of member churches has more than doubled and includes Christian churches from Africa, Asia, the Caribbean, Latin America, the Middle East, and the Pacific. Women, lay people, and youth are vitally involved in leadership roles in the World Council of Churches.

The council remains committed today to helping churches around the world share all their resources—human, spiritual, cultural, and material. It encourages churches to express their faith in energetic and effective action. During emergency situations, the WCC often takes an important leadership role in coordinating churches to respond. The council has also made a commitment to promote the vision of justice and peace.

In addition to the obvious benefits of working for justice, peace, and relief, the council's work is based on the concept of helping churches respect one another's strengths and needs and on recognizing and upholding each other's rights and responsibilities.

The World Council of Churches describes its goal today as a common spiritual journey towards visible unity. Beyond theological oneness, the council proclaims that the church must be an example of inclusiveness that receives the gifts of all and hears the call to action.

Churches that are not a part of the World Council of Churches have also sought to work together—especially in the arena of social action. Evangelicals and fundamentalists, who disagreed on points of theology with the Roman Catholic Church and with denominations that made up the World Council of Churches, made efforts to participate more fully in the worldwide church following their Lausanne Conference in 1974.

A second conference of evangelicals, Lausanne II, was held in Manila, the Philippines, in 1989. It heralded a new sense of unity among charismatics and non-charismatics. Roman Catholics and persons from the Orthodox faith were also welcomed at that gathering.

The "Manila Manifesto," an official document that resulted from Lausanne II, was sent to churches, not as a binding covenant but as an expression of commitments to be considered. The document asserted that social action was a part of preaching the kingdom of God and insisted that all members of Christ's body (including women and laity) be involved in witness. Cooperation in evangelism, "even with those communions that are not part of the evangelical movement," was also urged.

A spirit of cooperation also emerged toward the World Council of Churches. Following the conference, "the Lausanne Committee for World Evangelism was formed to encourage evangelicals to implement a global witness."[2]

The Roman Catholic Church also began ecumenical efforts following Vatican II, which convened in the fall of 1962. Pope John XXIII invited Protestant, Anglican, and Orthodox observers to attend the Vatican Council. New relationships emerged, and many new doors for dialogue and understanding opened. For example, when Vatican II began to allow the use of the common language rather than Latin for Mass, Catholic worship became much less foreign to non-Catholics. The Vatican Council also pronounced several areas such as economics, labor unions, nuclear weapons, and culture where Catholics and non-Catholics could work together despite their doctrinal differences. Although the Roman Catholic church is not a member of the World Council of Churches, it has established a strong working relationship with the WCC in areas of social service.

These steps toward unity have been relatively recent, but the urgent need for interdenominational cooperation in the United States dates back to changing social conditions after the Civil War.

A group of abolitionists, for example, organized a committee to defend a group of slaves that had mutinied aboard the slave ship *La Amistad* in 1838. The slaves were captured and imprisoned in Connecticut, but after lengthy trials the slaves were freed and returned to Africa in the care of three missionaries. The original committee that defended the slaves merged in 1846 with other anti-slavery societies to form the interdenominational American Missionary Association.

After the Civil War, this association, in cooperation with the government and the Freedmen's Bureau, built schools and churches for the newly freed slaves. Many colleges educating young African-Americans today trace their origins to the work of the missionaries of the American Missionary Association—schools like Talledaga College in Alabama, Tougaloo College in Mississippi, Fisk University in Tennessee, and Huston-Tillotson College in Texas.

In 1880, William Booth's British evangelistic movement, which came to be known as the Salvation Army, set up its first organization in the United States. Booth's original intention was to evangelize the poor in the slums, but he and his co-workers realized that they must also respond to the overwhelming needs of the persons they encountered. The Salvation Army set up shelters, soup kitchens, and simple dispensaries to take care of basic needs and also began job training and counseling programs. Although the Salvation Army has now become a distinct religious entity, Booth originally intended it to supplement the work of the churches, much as Habitat for Humanity seeks to be a servant of the churches.

Also in the early 1880s, the Reverend Albert Benjamin Simpson founded the Christian and Missionary Alliance made up of people of various denominations in the U.S. and Canada who supported overseas missions and set up many programs to help the poor in North America.

The rescue mission program was also established near the end of the nineteenth century. Missions and homes for outcast men and women were established in New York and Chicago. The movement soon spread to other cities.

The ecumenical movement in the United States has often been manifest in the role of educator. E. Talmadge Root, the first executive of the Federation of Churches movement in New England, said the churches should limit themselves to informing people about various issues. "Keep the facts before the people until the people change the facts," he said. In keeping with this philosophy, various interdenominational groups formed, issued proclamations, and presented ideas to the churches.

Leaders of many denominations, concerned about the distribution of wealth and the poor treatment of workers, urged reforms such as the abolition of child labor, reduction of the twelve-hour work day, and the assurance of one day of rest in seven.

Evangelists such as Billy Graham have brought together millions of Christians of different denominations and have encouraged them to work for the Lord.

Organizations like Campus Life, Intervarsity Christian Fellowship, Young Life, Campus Crusade for Christ, and the Fellowship of Christian

Athletes seek to evangelize and provide opportunities for their respective constituencies to serve.

In 1950, The National Council of Churches of Christ in the United States was formally organized by the union of several preexisting bodies, including the Federal Council of Churches (founded in 1908), the Foreign Missions Conference (organized in 1893), and the International Council of Religious Education. The National Council is a cooperative organization of which thirty-two Protestant and Orthodox churches are members, representing a constituency of about 47,000,000 people. It promotes cooperation among the churches and coordinates efforts on many matters, including famine relief, civil rights, world peace, and racial conflict. The council also supports member churches through Christian education, family life, home and foreign mission work, and broadcasting and films. Through the National Council, member churches are able to work with the worldwide community of fellow Christians to make a common witness to their faith, meet human need, protect the environment, and help bring peace and justice.

Habitat is in sympathy with the efforts of the World Council of Churches and other groups to influence churches and God's people to cooperate and work together. Habitat works with many churches that are not a part of the World Council or National Council, and those relationships are valued and deeply appreciated.

Habitat for Humanity is in agreement with the general purpose of the National Council of Churches, as we are with that of the World Council, but we are not a member of either. Our desire is that we be even more of a unifying force, bringing more churches—both at the national and international level and at the level of the local congregation—to work together even though there may be doctrinal differences. My sincere hope is that "the theology of the hammer" can transcend all barriers, and that we can get everybody working together!

The theology of unity, which drives so many of the interdenominational organizations mentioned in this chapter, and "the theology of the hammer," which is central in Habitat for Humanity, are totally compatible. My prayer is that we can work even more closely together, at all levels, and with more and more churches and church agencies in the months and years ahead. By doing so, the work and witness of everyone will be strengthened.

So, get out your hammers, Catholics and Protestants, liberals and conservatives, Reform and Orthodox, Unitarians and Trinitarians, Gentiles and Jews. We have some houses to build to the glory of God! "The theology of the hammer" binds us together in common ministry.

Notes

[1]Robert McAfee Brown, "Ecumenical Movement," *The Encyclopedia of Religion*, ed. Mircea Eliade, 16 vols. (New York: Macmillan, 1987) 18-26.

[2]Richard V. Pierard, "Luasane II: Reshaping World Evangelism," *The Christian Century* (16 August 1989) 741-42.

Two participants in the 1993 Collegiate Challenge work on a roof truss at Habitat's project site in Clarksdale, MS. A colleague's smile reflects the joy of partnering with people in need. (Photo by Julie Lopez)

Corporate partners have increasingly joined Habitat's work on a major scale, as exemplified by the 1992 Jimmy Carter Work Project in Washington, D.C., where ten houses—all sponsored by organizations—were built in one week.

Chapter 8

A Theology
Full of Partnerships

Previous chapters have covered the extensive partnerships Habitat enjoys with churches, church agencies, and other religious organizations. This chapter focuses on the plethora of partnerships Habitat for Humanity has with other groups.

Thousands of such partnerships have been entered into at the local level, with Habitat projects from Columbus, Georgia, to Khammam, India, and hundreds of towns and cities in between and beyond. Obviously, I cannot possibly write about even a significant fraction of these partnerships. I can attempt, however, to shed at least some light on some of the fantastic cooperative endeavors that have been negotiated by Habitat for Humanity International or by a consortium of local Habitat affiliates and that have meant, and continue to mean, so much to this ever-growing venture that puts faith and love into action and gives tangible meaning and fulfillment to "the theology of the hammer."

A whole passel of partnerships with the corporate world is taking on more significance all the time. These new relationships are most helpful in building more and more houses for needy families.

In January 1990, the very first corporate partnership that Habitat for Humanity International entered into, with the Southern Bell Company (BellSouth Telecommunications), was consummated. Frank Skinner, chairman and CEO of BellSouth at that time, was the driving force in making that partnership possible.

The ongoing partnership calls for the company to provide twenty-five percent of the money needed to build a Habitat house in a local community in its market area (nine Southeastern states). Local employees of the company raise another twenty-five percent of the cost and recruit volunteers to actually build the house. The local Habitat affiliate provides the remaining fifty percent of the money.

During the first three years of the partnership with BellSouth, fifty houses were sponsored by the company. More than 3,500 employees participated in the program. As reported in chapter one, the fiftieth house was built as a part of the 20/20,000 project in April 1993, and dedicated to Frank Skinner. Since that time, several more BellSouth houses have been built throughout the Southeast.

The largest corporate commitment to Habitat for Humanity to date was made by America's Favorite Chicken (AFC), the parent company for Popeyes Famous Fried Chicken and Biscuits and Churchs Chicken.

In late 1992, the chief executive officer of AFC, Frank Belatti, contacted Habitat for Humanity International and entered into negotiations with Jane Emerson in our development office. A man of decisive action and with a deep concern for the communities where his company has stores, Frank knew what he wanted to do—fully sponsor 100 Habitat houses to be built over a five-year period. That was a commitment of $3,500,000!

As we began to get acquainted with Frank Belatti, we realized that he was a man with vision and wanted to move. He was excited; so were we.

In January 1993, Frank attended the inauguration of Bill Clinton. He was so inspired by President Clinton's inaugural address that he wrote the President and promised to double the commitment of his company to Habitat for Humanity to 200 houses over five years—a $7,000,000 commitment! President Clinton forwarded Frank's letter to me with his own cover letter.

Shortly thereafter, Frank and his wife, Kathy, attended a weekend event with former President and Mrs. Carter at Habitat headquarters, along with a group of about twenty-five other special Habitat partners. Frank came with an armful of promotional materials he and his people had created for AFC's emerging partnership with Habitat. The new program, he had decided, would be called "Dream Builders."

By summer, Frank and his company were ready to build their first house. Since the new corporate headquarters were located in Atlanta, it was decided to build the house in partnership with Atlanta Habitat for Humanity. Ground was broken in June, and building began immediately. Nine weeks later it was finished and ready to be occupied by the proud and happy new homeowner, Lisa Jones.

Linda and I were privileged to be present for the very emotional dedication service for this first AFC house, which was held on Sunday afternoon, August 22, in the Mechanicsville neighborhood of south Atlanta. Frank and Kathy were there, of course, along with several other key leaders in the company, including Lucy White, project manager for the AFC-Habitat partnership, and Joe Genovese, AFC executive vice-president.

Lisa, a single mother, was there with her two boys, Rodney (thirteen months) and Vanion (three years). Also, the company had flown in the new homeowner-to-be for its second house, Paulette Brown, from San Antonio, Texas. Her house would be built in October as part of San Antonio Habitat for Humanity's "Miracle Week," a blitz-build of three houses.

Several people spoke at the dedication service, including Frank Belatti and myself. The emotional high point of the afternoon, however, was when Lisa spoke. She said it had long been her goal to be a homeowner and that today her dream was coming true. She cried a lot as she poured out her heart, and many others cried with her. All of the tears, though, were tears of incredible happiness and overflowing joy.

Following construction of the San Antonio house, the AFC partnership built six more houses in 1993—in New Orleans, Louisiana; Jackson, Mississippi; Washington, D.C.; Donna, Texas; and Tampa and Miami, Florida.

In January 1994, AFC blitz-built two houses in Dallas and Fort Worth in connection with its convention in Dallas. The company expects to build the remainder of its quota of forty houses in various locations around the country before the year's end.

Why did the company enter into this partnership with Habitat? Frank Belatti says simply,

> We believe that everyone deserves to have a safe and decent home for themselves and their children. Unfortunately, this is increasingly difficult—even for people with full time jobs. We wanted to do something to help, especially in the neighborhoods in which we live and work, and we were convinced that Habitat for Humanity was the right organization for us. We believe the relationship will be good for our company, good for Habitat for Humanity, good for local communities, and certainly good for the 1,000 or so people who will live in the 200 houses.

Jimmy Carter was responsible for a partnership with another fine company. In early 1992, at a meeting at the Carter Center in Atlanta, he introduced us to leaders of the National Gypsum Company. A commitment was made to help Habitat in various ways.

In 1992, the company furnished all the wallboard for the ten houses built during the Jimmy Carter project in Washington, D.C. In 1993, it provided all the wallboard for the 20/20,000 project in Americus, plus full sponsorship of one of the houses. Through its foundation, the company made a $50,000 contribution to Habitat International in 1993. National Gypsum also furnished all the wallboard for the 1993 blitz-build in Charlotte, North Carolina, and wallboard for the first six houses built in the wake of Hurricane Andrew in south Florida.

The Square D Company, headquartered in Chicago, is, with its parent company (Groupe Schneider of Paris, France), the global leader in electrical distribution systems. Since 1991, the company has been supporting Habitat for Humanity with donations of residential electrical distribution products. In 1992, the company donated enough equipment for 250 Habitat houses. In 1993, it gave equipment for 275 houses. Square D employees are active in many local Habitat affiliates and were involved with the 1991 and 1992 Jimmy Carter Work Projects. As reported in chapter one, the company sponsored one of the 20/20,000 houses in Americus.

Black & Decker Corporation, the world's largest producer of power tools and power accessories, has been a supporter of Habitat for several years as a part of its "Build a Better America" program.

Another manufacturer of power tools, Milwaukee Electric Tool Corporation, donated 950 tools worth $140,000 to Habitat for Humanity International in 1993 for distribution to local Habitat projects across the country.

Mannington Mills of Salem, New Jersey entered into partnership with Habitat in 1991. Since that time, the company has provided flooring for an estimated 1,000 Habitat houses.

Royal Rubber and Manufacturing Company, the nation's largest manufacturer of floor mats made of recycled tire rubber, is headquartered in South Gate, California. In October 1992, the company opened an east coast manufacturing plant in Calhoun, Georgia. At that time, Royal Rubber board chairman Eugene F. McClung, Jr., announced a partnership with Habitat for Humanity. Royal's partnership includes the donation of funds from sales of their Veldura ceramic tile pattern floor mat, a Green Cross certified product that is made of eighty percent recycled post-consumer rubber.[1]

J. Smith Lanier and Company, headquartered in West Point, Georgia (just across the border from my hometown of Lanett, Alabama), celebrated its 125th year of insuring people, homes, and businesses in January 1993. As a special way to observe this milestone, the company entered into a partnership with Habitat for Humanity to build houses in each community where the company has a branch office. Over the twelve months following the formation of this partnership, Habitat houses were built and dedicated in Auburn and Huntsville, Alabama; and in West Point, La Grange, Columbus, Carrollton, and Newnan, Georgia.

A partnership was launched in 1993, under the guidance of Jane Emerson and Marykate Wilson of our development department, with the United Consumers Club. Headquartered in Merrillville, Indiana, the UCC is a company that has a reputation of being "the best kept secret in America." Since 1971, United Consumers Club has been providing American consumers with a higher quality lifestyle by allowing them to obtain things they need for their families at prices they can afford. Currently, UCC has eighty-six franchises in twenty-five states, with plans to expand into Canada and Mexico.

In addition to directly benefiting members, United Consumers Club wants to reach out and make a positive impact on the communities where it has franchises. In the UCC/Habitat partnership, the goal is to help raise funds for building houses for needy families in cities where the franchises are located. In the first year of the UCC/Habitat partnership, $90,000 was given by UCC franchises to sixty-six different local Habitat affiliates. A great success in the first year has prompted a plan to duplicate the program in 1994, with the expectation that the money raised will be doubled!

In Florida, still another exciting partnership named "It takes you" was inaugurated in 1993. Initiated by WESH, Channel 2 T.V. in Orlando, the house blitz-building venture included six affiliates in the station's viewing area—Habitat for Humanity of Greater Apopka, Habitat for Humanity of Lake County, Habitat for Humanity of Greater Ocala, Space Coast Habitat for Humanity, Halifax Habitat for Humanity, and Habitat for Humanity in Seminole County—and, as contributors, Burger King, Lynx, Walt Disney World, and Home Depot. The first house was started on October 2, 1993. All six houses were completed and dedicated within one month.

Home Depot, incidentally, has also been a wonderful partner with Habitat in several other cities across the country. Suzanne Apple, director of community affairs, estimates that its involvement with all of the various affiliates is approaching $1,000,000 annually, making the company one of our largest corporate donors.

Our partnership with Larsen Manufacturing Company derived from a relationship with Twin Cities Habitat in Minneapolis-St. Paul. The company donated combination screen/storm doors. Soon thereafter, Dale Larsen, president of the company, took a strong personal interest in the work and felt involvement should be expanded beyond Minneapolis. The Gifts in Kind department at our headquarters was contacted and a nationwide program established. The company's high quality screen/storm doors are now being donated to local affiliates all across the United States—delivered at no cost!

Another partnership that originated in Minneapolis is with GMAC's Residential Funding Corporation (RFC). The genesis of this unique partnership was a luncheon in February 1991 where RFC's Mary Tingerthal asked Twin Cities executive director Stephen Seidel, "Is there a way we can leverage the properties you've already developed?" A positive response from Steve resulted in the creation of the "Homes First: Sharing the Dream®" program of RFC that provides long-term, no-interest or low-interest loans to Habitat affiliates. These loans are secured by liens that Habitat holds on the houses it has sold and financed. The benefit of this pioneering program is that it frees capital for the affiliate and enables the building of more houses at a faster pace. The plan in no way affects the central feature of Habitat of not charging interest to the Habitat homeowners. By the end of 1993, over $5,000,000 had been loaned to ten affiliates in Minnesota, North Carolina, Illinois, California, and Georgia.

Yet another wonderful partnership to originate in Minneapolis is with Target stores. In the summer of 1993, in cooperation with Twin Cities Habitat, the company sponsored a Habitat house that was built in the suburban town of Hopkins. Workers from twenty-six different Target stores in the Twin Cities area signed on to build it. Over 700 employees—from store cashiers to corporate executives—volunteered to help Diane and Tony O'Brien and their three young daughters have a new home. The house was completed in October. The experience was such a good one that it was expanded and became known as Target's "Building a Wonderful Life" campaign. Ann Aronson, marketing manager and community relations expert with the company, said that every time a new Target store is opened, Target will build a Habitat home nearby.

Ryland Homes and Mortgage Company, headquartered in Columbia, Maryland, began working with Habitat for Humanity in early 1994. The company expects to help Habitat affiliates in all of its forty locations to fund local house-building projects. The program includes full sponsorship, supplier support, and executive leadership at the affiliate level.

Centex Homes, the giant home building organization headquartered in Dallas, Texas, has sponsored literally scores of Habitat houses all over the United States for several years. Their faithful and very generous support is tremendously appreciated.

In Canada, Habitat for Humanity has developed an impressive array of corporate partnerships. One of the most important is with Westroc Industries Limited of Mississauga, Ontario. Donald Leask, president and CEO of this fine company, committed drywall and related finishing materials to the houses in both Winnipeg and Kitchener for the Jimmy Carter work projects in July 1992. The company also contributed in several other significant ways during that year. The company has promised continuing support, including drywall for up to seventy-five houses in 1994 and 5,000 t-shirts for the Ed Schreyer blitz-build in the summer of 1994. (Ed Schreyer, a member of the board of directors of Habitat for Humanity of Canada, is a former premier of Manitoba and former Governor-General of Canada.)

Other corporate partnerships in Canada include:

• Aikenhead's Home Improvement Warehouse. This company and its president, Stephen Bebis, have given tremendous support in a number of ways.

• Delta Faucet and company president, Michael Campbell, provided the plumbing fixtures for all Habitat houses in Canada in 1993, and agreed to do the same in 1994.

• In 1993, Emco Limited built the first Habitat house in London, Ontario, in celebration of the 200th birthday of the city. The company also provided shingles for forty Habitat houses across Canada in the same year.

• Alexanian Carpets provided the flooring for all Habitat houses in Ontario in 1993, and have made a commitment to do the same in 1994.

• Dupont provided the house wrap for all Habitat houses in Canada in 1993, and indications are that the gift will be repeated in 1994 and beyond.

• The Canadian Imperial Bank of Commerce makes an annual $10,000 contribution to Habitat of Canada and encourages all of its branches across Canada to accept donations from any customers for Habitat. As this book goes to press, negotiations are underway with the Royal Bank of Canada to support Habitat's work.

Several other significant corporate partners in Canada are being added all the time. Gratitude and profound appreciation are my sentiments about this growing and very generous support of Habitat's work in Canada. It is enabling the work there to grow and expand in a most impressive way.

One of the most exciting and fruitful partnerships in the United States is with Gifts In Kind America (GIKA). This specialized non-profit organization solicits products from corporations across the country and directs these products to non-profit groups that need them. Thousands of dollars worth of building materials, computer software, and office supplies have been channeled to Habitat for Humanity International and to hundreds of local affiliates. The largest such donation was a gift of insulation valued at more than $1,000,000 from the Owens Corning Company. Susan Corrigan, the talented president of GIKA, has also introduced Habitat to other non-profit groups that are proving beneficial to our expanding work. Finally, Gifts In Kind America has created a "Housing America Initiative" that has the specific mandate of soliciting and distributing building materials to non-profit organizations. Habitat for Humanity is the principal beneficiary of that program.

Other partnerships that are proving to be so vital to the growing work of Habitat for Humanity are with associations, fraternal organizations, and civic groups. These highly valued partnerships give greater meaning and purpose to "the theology of the hammer."

Without a doubt, one of the most important and deeply appreciated partnerships we have is with the National Association of Home Builders (NAHB). For years, local home builders associations have aided Habitat affiliates with funding, materials, and, above all, expertise. In 1992, the NAHB helped Habitat affiliates throughout the nation as a part of its "Homes Across America" program. Scores of Habitat houses were built as a part of this initiative. *Builder* magazine, the official publication for the

NAHB, also raised thousands of dollars for the work both in 1992 and 1993.

Another very special partnership is with the National Fraternal Congress of America (NFCA). (See chapter six.) It was entered into as a result of the work of Ed Lindell, senior vice president of external affairs of Lutheran Brotherhood and now a member of the board of Habitat International. In 1990, Ed was chairman of the "Cause Committee" of the NFC. He and his colleague, John Bookout, president of Woodmen of the World, contacted me and, after a thorough investigation, recommended to their board that Habitat for Humanity be adopted as a national cause. This partnership has been a rich and rewarding one for both the member fraternals and Habitat for Humanity.

Yet another partnership that is still quite new but holds great promise is that with Elderhostel. Their capable president, Bill Berkeley, came to Americus in December 1991 to work out the partnership arrangement with Habitat. The first groups of these retired, but very active, people from Elderhostel worked in Americus and at three other Habitat sites: Coahoma, Mississippi; Yakima, Washington; and Preston, West Virginia. Each Elderhostel group stays for two weeks. Participants pay for their lodging plus an amount to cover the cost of building materials.

A truly historic partnership is that between Habitat for Humanity and Delta Sigma Theta Sorority, one of the largest African-American women's organizations in the world. Led by its dynamic president, Dr. Bertha Roddey, this outstanding sorority adopted Habitat for Humanity as a major part of its social action program for the 1990s. The partnership was developed and is being nurtured by the campus chapters and diversity programs departments of Habitat for Humanity International. The recently organized diversity programs department is assigned to recruit, nurture, and incorporate new partnerships between racially and culturally diverse groups and Habitat for Humanity.

In 1993, the sorority raised funds and provided volunteers for building Habitat houses in each of its seven regions in the country: Southern Region—house built with Greater Miami Habitat for Humanity; Midwestern Region—house built with Greater Cleveland, Ohio Habitat; Central Region—house built with Kansas City, Missouri Habitat; Far West Region—house built with Los Angeles Habitat for Humanity in Linwood, California; Eastern Region—house built with Camden, New Jersey Habitat; South Atlantic Region—house built with Greater Greensboro Habitat of Greensboro, North Carolina; and Southwest Region—house built with Greater Albuquerque, New Mexico Habitat.

The Southern Region, in addition to building the house with Greater Miami Habitat for Humanity, has already awarded a $10,000 seed grant to its Nassau, Bahamas, chapter to start the first Habitat affiliate in that country!

Future plans call for Delta Sigma Theta to build or rehabilitate fifteen houses at the site of the sorority's forty-second national convention in the St. Louis, Missouri/East St. Louis, Illinois, area and dedicate those houses at the national convention, July 17-23, 1994, as a part of "The Road to L. A." program I described in chapter five.

In subsequent years, Delta Sigma Theta plans to sponsor the building of Habitat houses in a developing country in Africa, including sending volunteers in 1995 to work on the houses, building or rehabilitating a house in 1996 in each state where the organization has chapters, and producing a documentary video in 1997 on the ongoing efforts of local chapters to eliminate poverty housing in their communities.

Delta Sigma Theta, Dr. Bertha Roddey, and all of her dedicated and talented associates are a wonderful blessing to the growing work of Habitat for Humanity. We thank God for every one of them!

A more limited partnership, but one that we hope will grow, is with Alpha Phi Alpha. This group, which is the oldest African-American fraternity in the country, helped build a Habitat house in New Orleans in connection with its eighty-seventh annual convention in August 1993.

Communications have begun with other African-American sororities, fraternities, denominations, and organizations to join Habitat for Humanity International in its goal of eliminating poverty housing. A strong interest and commitment have been voiced among minority professionals to become actively involved with Habitat for Humanity and to not only build houses but to build lives and communities through this ministry.

As indicated earlier, our campus chapters department works with college or university groups in addition to over 300 official campus chapters of Habitat for Humanity. We are so grateful for the many partnerships that have evolved over the past few years between these dedicated campus groups and Habitat affiliates across the nation and in several other countries. Those students certainly do know how to put "the theology of the hammer" into practice.

The campus chapters department has also assumed responsibility for guiding an emerging new partnership—prison chapters of Habitat for Humanity.

Over 1,000,000 Americans are now in prison. The United States has the highest per capita incarceration rate in the world. More African-American young men are in prison than in college. Surely, we, as a society, and Habitat, as a ministry, should reach out to these neighbors and try to help them have a better life.

For many years and in many places, prisoners have worked on Habitat houses. In Mississippi, especially, prisoners have worked at

Habitat construction sites. We have also worked with Chuck Colson's Prison Fellowship ministry over the years in numerous places. In 1986, Chuck himself, along with a dozen prisoners, worked with the Jimmy Carter project in Chicago.

A formal program was never in place for organizing this aspect of our work. Then, in November 1991, I was in Chicago to speak at the annual meeting of Lutheran Social Services of Illinois. As I visited with the people after my talk, I was approached by Jack Nordgaard, Illinois state director of the Lutherans' prisoner and family ministry. "Why don't you have a program for prisoners to work in Habitat?" he asked.

"Because you haven't started it!" I replied.

Jack accepted the challenge. Over the coming months, he worked with the campus chapters department in Americus to establish the procedures for this new dimension of Habitat's work. The first group to form was at the Kankakee minimum security unit for women. This unit is an extension of the Illinois state women's prison at Dwight. Inmates at the unit are close to being released. The women work with Pembroke Habitat for Humanity in renovating houses. The program is a win-win deal: Habitat benefits from the donated labor, and the inmates benefit by enhanced self-esteem and improved chances for employment in the future due to construction skills they have learned. Other chapters have now been formed or cooperative programs are underway in several other locations.

An extensive series of partnerships in Habitat for Humanity is with civic clubs, especially Rotary, Kiwanis, Junior Chambers of Commerce, and Junior Leagues. When one takes a look at the slogans of these clubs, it is no surprise that the clubs would be attracted to Habitat for Humanity. The Rotarians, for example, have as their motto, "Service above self"—a match with Habitat!

One of the most moving experiences I have ever had was in connection with a house built by a Rotary Club in Bend, Oregon. Linda and I had been invited to Bend, a small town in central Oregon with a really dynamic Habitat project that had been founded by Les Alford (who now serves as area director for the West, Northwest, and Rocky Mountain Habitat regions). One of our responsibilities there was to participate in dedicating two newly completed houses, one sponsored and built by the local Rotary Club.

Our plane was a little late so it was necessary for us to go directly to the site of the two houses as quickly as possible. The service of dedication was already underway when we arrived. As the service progressed, one of the local project leaders brought to us the two families who would live in the houses. A beautiful little eight year-old girl with blond hair, named Jamie, would move into the house built by the Rotary Club. Right away, Jamie and I became friends. She was a very vivacious little girl, full of life.

In a few minutes, I was called to speak. As I talked, I looked over at my new friend, Jamie. She was beaming. Spontaneously, I called to her, and she came running with a big smile on her face.

I took Jamie into my arms and faced her toward the crowd. "Jamie," I said, "these people have come here today to dedicate these two houses, but, really, they came to show their love for you and your family and the other family. What do you think about that, Jamie?"

"I like it!" she exclaimed.

I continued, "Jamie, they tell me your family and the other family will move into your new houses day after tomorrow. Is that right?"

"Yes," she responded.

"Jamie, what is it about your new house that you like best?"

"Our family will be together and I'm going to have my own room." she replied.

The crowd loved it. I put Jamie down. She returned to her parents and I finished my speech.

As I was mingling in the crowd afterwards, a man touched me on the shoulder and said, "Millard, that was beautiful what you did with Jamie. Has anyone told you where that family has been living?"

"No," I replied.

"Millard, Jamie's family has been living under a bridge!"

Little girls should not have to live under a bridge. Thank God, and thanks to the generosity of the Rotary Club in Bend, that precious little girl no longer has to live under a bridge. She has her own room and is blossoming like a rose into a beautiful and special young woman.

In working with Habitat for Humanity in Bend and many other places, the Rotarians surely are living up to their slogan as they build more and more houses for people like Jamie.

The slogan for the Kiwanis Club is, "We Build." How could they not be interested in *building* houses for needy families?

The Junior Chamber of Commerce (Jaycees) has a creed that reads, in part, "We believe that faith in God gives meaning and purpose to human life, that the brotherhood of man transcends the sovereignty of nations, and that service to humanity is the best work of life." All across the land, Jaycees are supporting Habitat by providing volunteers, donating money, and sometimes sponsoring a whole house, or, in some places, several houses. In Greensboro, North Carolina, the Jaycees sponsored a whole street of Habitat houses. The money was largely raised through golf tournaments.

The Association of Junior Leagues proclaims, "where a woman can change the world." Many women, through the Junior League, have certainly been changing the world for many needy families by partnering with Habitat affiliates across the country to build houses. The Junior

League of Jackson, Mississippi, has been especially helpful with the Habitat affiliate in that city. The League has been equally supportive in Lynchburg, Virginia.

Linda and I were in Lynchburg some months ago after the Junior League members had just completed "their" Habitat house. We had the privilege of taking part in the dedication service. I was touched to see the love and respect that had grown between the Junior League members and the Habitat homeowner family.

Other civic clubs are also supporting Habitat, though I cannot list all of them. When these clubs are contacted for support, we cite the organization's creed or slogan. Habitat simply provides an opportunity for the clubs to live out and observe what they stand for.

While women's groups like the Junior League and Pilot Club are already supportive of Habitat, there is a movement afoot to bring women together from all walks of life to build Habitat houses.

The idea originated in Charlotte, North Carolina, in 1990. At a luncheon in November, immediately following the dedication of Charlotte's 100th house, someone asked, "What can we do next, as an encore?" Darlene Jonas, a family support volunteer with Charlotte Habitat, answered with an intriguing question, "Wouldn't we have enough talent to build a house entirely by women?" The response was immediate, enthusiastic, and totally positive.

Ruth Martin, a long-time and very dedicated Habitat volunteer builder, was one of those present at the luncheon. She surmised that they could get Rosalynn Carter to join them. On the spot, she was commissioned to invite her. A letter went out to Rosalynn, who responded positively to the idea, and planning kicked into high gear.

Susan Hancock, executive director of Charlotte Habitat at the time, remembers being extremely tired when the idea surfaced. "But," she recalls, "that night I couldn't sleep just thinking about the exciting possibilities."

The project was named "Look, Look! See Jane Build!" Full-time volunteer Mary Olive Johnson, a superb organizer and skilled architect, agreed to coordinate the construction. Two professional women in the construction trade, Clara Faulk and Jill Frazier, accepted the challenge of teaching and advising unskilled women how to do the necessary tasks.

The Woman's Council of Charlotte's Home Builders Association began soliciting donations of building materials. Others began to raise the needed funds for the pioneering project.

Actual planning for the building of the house started in February 1991. Women were in charge of every phase. Over 500 women became involved in the project in one way or another. (The women did allow men to bring snacks and prepare some of the meals! And, of course, the building inspector, a man, had to come on site, but he agreed to wear a wig!)

Women dug the footers, poured and leveled the slab, then were ready for the big two-day blitz in May to erect the walls and mount the trusses.

Rosalynn Carter was there for the exciting first day. Women from the Charlotte Ministerial Association led the opening worship. Then, the walls went up!

By the end of the second day, the windows and doors had been installed, and felt was on the roof.

Siding and drywall were installed in June, and interior finishing work, including painting, was done in late June and July. The finished house was dedicated in August.

Linda was privileged to be the speaker at the dedication service. I was allowed to introduce her, but that was the extent of what I was permitted to do! (The excited new homeowner, Janet Stewart, moved in a few days later with her two daughters, Tanita and Shameka. They would never forget the uniqueness of their beautiful new home!)

The successful project in Charlotte quickly spawned other such initiatives. The second "all women built house" was in Minneapolis, sponsored by Twin Cities Habitat for Humanity.

Habitat leaders there decided to run a notice in local publications inviting interested women to come to an organization meeting:

**It's time for women to put on
their aprons and start doing some housework.**

And we don't mean scrubbing and dusting. Beginning Mother's Day weekend, an all-female team of volunteers will build a house with a low-income woman and her family, in the Phillips neighborhood of Minneapolis. We're calling it The Constructive Women's Project–a special program of Habitat For Humanity, designed to build the skills, self-esteem, and sense of community of everyone who participates. Right now, our single greatest need is raising the money to buy materials. We're also looking for both skilled and unskilled women to contribute their labor and for men to contribute child care and meals. So if you'd like to help call 333-3372. This is one form of housework that lasts.

They expected maybe 150 women to respond. Imagine their amazement when over 400 women showed up! The project was on. A goal was set to raise enough money for one house. The motivated women quickly raised $63,000!

The Constructive Women's Project started actual building in May 1992. The house was finished and dedicated in February 1993. A very happy Tami Cumber and her four children—Monique, Brianna, Kia, and Cory, Jr.—moved in, full of joy about their beautiful new, all-women-built, house.

A month after the house was started in Minneapolis, women of the American Legion Auxiliary built one of the ten houses in the Jimmy Carter blitz-building week in Washington, D.C.

The women-built house idea came to Americus as the result of a week of services led by women during our regular morning devotional time at our international headquarters. Long-time volunteer Tilly Grey and former International Partner and current staff member Bonnie Watson were concerned about lack of opportunities in Americus for women to have leadership roles in Habitat's mission, so they lined up thirty-four women to participate in devotions that week. That was not enough, however.

When the Sumter County Initiative was announced, women at headquarters wanted to help, but they did not know exactly how. During a lunch time walk, Bonnie Watson and Carol Gregory (assistant director of U.S. affiliate work) came up with the idea of building a house entirely by the work of women.

Bonnie and Tilly became co-chairs of the house-building effort, with good help from Habitat volunteer Julianne Crane who had excellent organizational skills. After much debate, the name W.A.T.C.H. (Women Accepting the Challenge of Housing) was chosen for the project.

Funds were raised in a variety of ways, and detailed plans were made to build the first house. Before that pioneering house got underway, a "training house" was built with several men on the local construction crew teaching the women needed skills. The person chosen to lead the project was Elizabeth Earle—a young, vivacious volunteer from Winston-Salem, North Carolina.

Construction got underway in November 1992. The W.A.T.C.H. house was the first fully sponsored house in the Sumter County Initiative. After four months, the house was finished and ready for dedication and occupancy by Sandra Bryant and her three children—Meghan, Miriam, and Brian.

Mildred Burton, who, with her husband, Perry, had received a partnership house at Koinonia Farm twenty years earlier, helped extensively with the construction of the W.A.T.C.H. house. She wrote a poem about the experience and read it at the dedication service. This is what she penned:

> Who Am I?
> I am a student and I am a teacher.
> I am a learner and I am a leader.
> I am a mother and I am a daughter.
>   Who am I? (A woman of W.A.T.C.H.)
> I am a companion and I am a friend.
> I am weak and I am strong.
> I am a wife and I am a sweetheart.

I am young and I am old.
> Who am I? (A woman of W.A.T.C.H.)
I am wise and I am foolish.
I am equal and I am an opposite.
I am an adult and I am a child.
I am plain and I am beautiful.
> Who am I? (A woman of W.A.T.C.H.)
I am single and I am married.
I am widowed and I am divorced.
I am simple and I am complex.
I am a housewife and I am a career girl.
> Who am I? (A woman of W.A.T.C.H.)

A second W.A.T.C.H. house was announced at the dedication of the first one. It was built at the Hope Community (site of the 20/20,000 project). Franciscan Order Sisters, Teri Wall and Francine Schwarzenberger, served as co-leaders of that house, which was dedicated in November 1993. (A second "training house" was built immediately after the first house dedication in order to teach more women how to build. Teri and Francine were the leaders of that house to prepare themselves and other women for the building of the second W.A.T.C.H. house.) A third W.A.T.C.H. house was built in 1994.

Other Habitat affiliates with houses built by women include Atlanta, Georgia ("Women Helping Women Coalition"—involving ten different women's groups.); Denver, Colorado ("W.A.T.C.H."); Houston, Texas ("The Women's House for Habitat"); Fresno, California ("The Woman Built House"); South Hampton Roads, Virginia ("The House that Jill Built"); Bend, Oregon ("Women Hammer for Habitat"); South Brevard, Florida ("Junior League of South Brevard"); Cleveland, Ohio ("See Jane Build"); Columbus, Ohio ("The Habitat Women's House"); Canton, Ohio ("W.A.T.C.H."); Jackson, Mississippi ("The Junior League of Jackson"); Greensboro, North Carolina ("All-Women's House"); Asheville, North Carolina ("The Women Attorneys of Buncombe"); Sumter, South Carolina ("The Women's Project"); San Antonio, Texas ("The Woman's House"); Austin, Texas ("All Women-Built House"); and Ft. Smith, Arkansas ("Belle's Building Brigade").

Habitat groups in Alabama, Indiana, and Kentucky regularly feature all-women work days when women come to hammer and learn as they contribute to building a house.

Lexington, Kentucky Habitat for Humanity completed an all-women house in early 1994, with the workers including women from the federal women's prison in Lexington. One of the inmates had experience in heating systems and led the crew that installed the furnace. All the women inmates enjoyed the experience—so much so that they sponsored a Christmas party at the work site!

As this book goes to press, plans are being made for all-women-built houses in Sioux Falls, South Dakota; Sun City, Arizona; Lafayette, Indiana; St. Louis, Missouri; Knoxville, Tennessee; Salisbury, North Carolina; Hartford, Connecticut; Kansas City, Kansas; Cape Cod, Massachusetts; and several other locations. Country music artist Reba McEntire agreed to fund the construction of a house built entirely by women in Nashville. In making the commitment, she said she was eager to hammer nails with other women volunteers, because she wanted her involvement to be more than "Reba writes a check." The house got underway in January 1994.

Many affiliates that have built one or two houses by women are planning to build still more, and a group has been formed to build the first all-women-built house in Manila, the Philippines!

In Greensboro, as the All-Women's House was going up, senior Girl Scouts were building a Habitat house, the first in the nation to be built by Girl Scouts. They raised all the money for the house and built it with the help of their parents, boyfriends, and the homeowners. For this great effort, each member of the troop earned a "Gold Award," the highest award given to a Girl Scout. On December 11, 1993, with Linda and me participating in the celebration, this "Girl Scout House" became the 25,001st house built by Habitat for Humanity International, following by only a few hours the dedication of the 25,000th house in Charlotte.

The Sisters of Loretto, a Roman Catholic order of nuns, are making plans to construct a "nun-built house" in connection with their 1994 annual meeting in St. Louis. If successful, their intention is to make such a build a regular feature of their annual gatherings.

As all these projects were being planned by female Habitat partners, a very male-oriented partnership got underway in the spring of 1993. I received a phone call from my good friend Ken Henson, Jr., an outstanding young lawyer who serves as president of the Habitat affiliate in Columbus, Georgia. He was calling to tell me that John Turner of "The Game" wanted to talk to me. Ken explained that "The Game" was a division of the W. C. Bradley Company, which is headquartered in Columbus, and that they furnished some of the paraphernalia—such as hats, sweat shirts, t-shirts, and so forth—that are sold at professional football games and in many stores. Ken said that John wanted his division, in cooperation with the National Football League (NFL) and other suppliers, to sponsor some Habitat houses in connection with the 1994 Super Bowl game that would be played in Atlanta in January.

I called John immediately. He reminded me that we had met briefly when I had spoken at his church, St. Luke's United Methodist, a couple of years earlier. He told me that there was, indeed, a serious interest in building four or five Habitat houses near the stadium in the days prior to the game, and that some of the players could participate in building them.

I told John that we would certainly cooperate with him and the other responsible parties to make it happen. I assured him that we had a very good Habitat organization in Atlanta, and that Larry Arney, the executive director, was one of the best Habitat leaders in the country. I explained that he would need to work directly with Atlanta Habitat and that I would have Larry Arney call him.

In the months following, and after many consultations involving Larry, representatives of NFL Properties and David Snell (director of Habitat's education ministries) and other staff members of Habitat for Humanity International, the deal was made. The official name of the project would be "The NFL Super Bowl XXVIII Habitat Blitz-Build."

The final decision was to build four houses, jointly sponsored by the NFL, "The Game," and "Stadium Stuff" (a retail outlet store in the Atlanta area). Land was found near the stadium, plans were agreed on for the houses, families were selected, and—during the last ten days of January, just prior to the Super Bowl—the houses were built. Linda and I were there for part of the blitz-building. We were joined by members of the four new homeowner families; Miss America, Kimberly Aiken; well-known political leader Jack Kemp, who is a former professional football player and a member of Habitat for Humanity International's board of directors; our son, Chris, and his wife, Dianne; several NFL players; and, of course, the dedicated staff of builders with Atlanta Habitat and many of their faithful volunteers.

Throughout the ten days of the blitz-building, radio, television, newspapers, and other publications gave extensive publicity.

During the three days prior to the Super Bowl game, Habitat was a part of the "NFL Experience," a sort of football theme park in the World Congress Center that provided interactive opportunities for visitors to be a part of the Super Bowl activities. We were given booth space in which a Habitat house was partially constructed. Designed by a creative team at Georgia Institute of Technology in Atlanta, three video touch-screen monitors were placed in the "house," allowing visitors to "build" a Habitat house on the screen by answering football trivia questions. Tote bags were given out with information about Habitat for Humanity. An estimated 100,000 people saw the Habitat display; at least 10,000 "built" Habitat houses on the video screens.

Also during the last week of the blitz-build, the popular ABC television series "Home Improvement" shot scenes for an episode that aired on March 9, giving tremendous additional exposure to the work of Habitat for Humanity.

The four completed Habitat houses were dedicated on Friday, January 28. That evening we had a joyous Habitat celebration at Antioch Baptist Church North, which is located just a block from the construction site. Following that service, which was attended by several hundred people, we had a candlelight procession from the church to the building site, where prayers of dedication were offered. The next day, all four families moved into their brand new houses. The following evening they enjoyed the Super Bowl game from the comfort of their new living rooms.

About the time John Turner was calling to tell me about the proposed partnership with Habitat in connection with the Super Bowl, another event of a very different sort was about to begin. Bill Harris, Jr., of Americus, Georgia; James Jackson of nearby Plains; Sue Tilson of Morristown, Tennessee (who had been serving as a volunteer in Americus); and Elizabeth Earle of Winston-Salem, North Carolina (supervisor for the first W.A.T.C.H house) decided to ride bicycles on a meandering 4,000-mile route from Americus to Winnipeg, Manitoba, Canada, to participate in the Jimmy Carter work project. This dedicated foursome left Americus a week after the 20/20,000 project. They first rode south, then turned north in Pensacola, Florida, and headed to Maine. From there they rode west to Minneapolis where they were joined by seventy-five more bicyclists. This greatly enlarged group rode north to Winnipeg, arriving there on Sunday, July 18, just at the beginning of the big building blitz. The group received a welcome appropriate for heroes. Jimmy and Rosalynn Carter were so caught up in the spirit of the exciting arrival that they personally gave the bicyclists $500 for Habitat's work. Another man in the crowd gave $1,000. In all, the combined group of bicyclists netted $63,000 for Habitat's work in the United States, Canada, and overseas.

As this book is going to press, some of these same bicyclists and others are planning a bicycle ride from Minneapolis to Eagle Butte, South Dakota, to arrive at the beginning of the project there in July 1994. Also, my good friend Bo Turner (pastor, author, counselor, and former mayor of Clarkesville, Georgia) plans to ride his bicycle across the United States from east to west in the summer of 1994 to raise funds for Habitat. He has invited interested persons to join him. The ride is to celebrate his sixtieth birthday and retirement from his career as a counselor at Clarkesville High School.

Yet another bike ride to benefit Habitat for Humanity is one being planned by students from five New Haven, Connecticut universities: Yale, Southern Connecticut State, Quinnipiac College, Albertus Magnus College, and the University of New Haven. The bikers plan to ride coast to coast, from New Haven to San Francisco, via Washington, D.C., leaving June 1 and traveling for ten weeks and covering 5,000 miles.

A whole network of partnerships that is absolutely central to this ministry is within the Habitat for Humanity organization itself. The Habitat for Humanity International board of directors, for example, is composed of twenty-nine committed people who give tirelessly of their time, talent, and resources to guide this work. Official board meetings are held three times a year at different locations throughout the world. Most board members travel to these meetings at their own expense. Edgar Stoesz, our dedicated chairman, routinely spends hundreds of hours in leading the board and especially in guiding us in the crucial matter of how best to govern the ever-expanding work of Habitat for Humanity.

Over 20,000 people serve on local and national Habitat for Humanity boards of directors around the world. Again, these committed people serve without pay and give literally thousands of hours of their time to direct Habitat's work in their respective areas.

The staff of over 300 people (including paid personnel and volunteers) at Habitat for Humanity's international headquarters in Americus constantly goes beyond the required hours of service to assure a smooth running organization. The staff members for our fifteen regional centers in the United States and area and national offices are on the job giving of themselves in truly selfless ways.

The most incredible and invaluable partnership of all is that with the hundreds of thousands of volunteers across the country and around the world who raise money, send newsletters, answer telephones, order building materials, drive nails, and saw boards to actually build and renovate the houses. These folks are the true heroes of Habitat for Humanity—people like LeRoy Troyer, who has served as Jimmy Carter's house leader and boss on every Jimmy Carter Work Project since 1986, and who has served on Habitat's international board of directors; Hub Erickson, who worked tirelessly to help make the fifteenth anniversary celebration in Columbus, Ohio (in 1991) a great success, and who goes all over the country to help wherever needed, in addition to aiding the Habitat affiliates in his native Chicago area; and the "Habitat Gypsies," who travel in their recreational vehicles to Habitat sites all over the country to lend helping hands as needed. These dedicated partners, led by Jack and Lois Wolters of Columbus, North Carolina, are a growing force for good in this ministry. I wish I could acknowledge the contributions of everyone, but that would take a volume of books! I thank God for every dedicated person who makes Habitat for Humanity work.

Finally, a partnership of great importance to Habitat for Humanity is that with government at all levels—local, state or provincial, and national. We have always sought to work in harmony with governmental authorities. Indeed, the good will of government is essential to the success of our work.

We have, however, from the beginning, put limits on the partnership with government. Simply stated, we have called upon governmental units at various levels to "set the stage," so that Habitat, with private funds, can build on that stage.

What we mean by "setting the stage" is: (1) providing land as a grant or at a nominal price; (2) donating or selling at a reduced price houses or apartment complexes that have fallen into disrepair; and (3) putting in streets, sidewalks, and services. In other words, we look to governments to prepare the way so that Habitat volunteers—using donated materials or materials purchased with donations from churches, civic and other organizations, companies, foundations, or individuals—can build or renovate houses for needy families.

All such funds, property, or services from government or units of government are accepted by Habitat for Humanity International or local Habitat affiliates, provided no strings are attached that violate Habitat principles.

The rationale for this policy is that, first of all, Habitat for Humanity always has been and wishes to remain a vibrant, viable, dynamic grass-roots movement of people motivated by faith and love, reaching out to help those in need to have a decent place to live on terms they can afford to pay. We do not want to overload the system with "easy money" from government that would have the effect of squelching the spirit of our incredible network of donors and volunteers.

Jesus said that it is more blessed to give than to receive. I believe that. Preserving this feature of giving in Habitat, in materials or money and personally, should never be compromised.

Also, Habitat for Humanity is "openly and unashamedly" a Christian movement. At all house dedication services Bibles are presented, hymns are sung, prayers are offered, messages are delivered, and homeowners and others are called upon to witness to their faith (if they so choose). At international headquarters in Americus, as has been reported elsewhere, each work day is started with a devotional service. Every work day at Jimmy Carter blitz-building projects is started with a devotion, including hymns and prayers. All around the world, devotions and other expressions of our reliance upon God permeate the ministry of Habitat for Humanity.

We would never want to become so entangled with or reliant upon government that our freedom to express our religious beliefs would be compromised.

Habitat for Humanity has always had a policy of building for needy people, regardless of race or religion, and we welcome donors and volunteers from all backgrounds and from whatever motivation. We are a religiously-driven, God-centered venture, however, that seeks to give tangible expression to God's love in all that we do.

A growing number of partnerships, with government and many other groups and individuals, enhances and enables us to keep building an ever increasing number of houses with and for God's people in need.

As we build these thousands of houses, through the many partnerships discussed, we must always be sure they are of good quality. "Simple and decent," which describes Habitat houses, does not mean "inferior." To the contrary, Habitat emphasizes quality of construction and high standards for building. We also stress the importance of building up people even as the houses are being constructed. (We now turn our attention to these important subjects in the following chapter.)

Note

[1]For more information about Green Cross, see chapter 9, page 119.

"All together now," says a work crew intent on getting a roofing truss up to waiting workers above as work progressed on the first all-women's house built in Americus.

Like any good construction team, President Clinton and First Lady Hilary Clinton—at the time both campaigning—work together on the Habitat house in Atlanta.
(Photo by Kimberly Prenda)

Senior volunteer workers form one of the most endearing and energetic partnerships in Habitat's worldwide outreach. Here veteran construction worker Johnny Gallo enjoys cheerful moments with a youngster during the 1993 Jimmy Carter Work Project in Winnipeg, Canada.
(Photo by Julie Lopez)

Chapter 9

A Well-Built Theology

As stated in chapter one, "the theology of the hammer" acknowledges that faith and love must be expressed to be complete. Simply talking or praying about faith and singing or chanting about love are deficient from a spiritual point of view, even though talking, praying, singing, or chanting are legitimate expressions of one's devotion to God.

Furthermore, implicit in the mandate to act is the scriptural requirement to perform such action in accordance with God's will and way. That will and way are clearly pointed toward perfection. In Deuteronomy 32:4 we read, "He is the Rock, his works are perfect." Samuel proclaimed, "As for God, his way is perfect" (2 Sam 22:31), and continued, "It is God who arms me with strength and makes my way perfect" (2 Sam 22:33). Jesus said, "Be perfect, therefore, as your heavenly Father is perfect" (Matt 5:48).

In Habitat for Humanity we constantly strive for perfection in all we do—building and renovating houses, interacting with donors and volunteers, and working with homeowners—in obedience to these and similar scriptures. We often do not succeed, but we strive to do whatever we are doing *right*.

This striving for perfection is a part of what we in Habitat call "the economics of Jesus," and it is an integral part of "the theology of the hammer."[1]

Jesus' many acts of healing are examples of perfection. He never partially or imperfectly healed anyone. He never said to a person, "Look, I'm on a tight schedule today. I have time for that right leg, but you'll just have to keep dragging the left one." Neither did he say to a blind person, "I'll restore sight to one eye, but I just don't have the time or desire to heal you completely." No! Every healing was complete and perfect. That is God's will and way. In like manner, Jesus dealt with situations of need in a complete and perfect way. Consider the feeding of the multitude. He took available resources—five pieces of bread and two fish—and fed all the people.

As I was growing up in Alabama, my father would often admonish me, when he saw me rushing through a job and not doing it as it should be done, "Anything worth doing at all is worth doing right." That was a profoundly religious statement, totally in line with the life and teaching of Jesus. In building houses for low-income families, we at Habitat always emphasize quality work. The houses should be simple, modest, and inexpensive, but not cheap nor shoddily built.

Several times a year, we have groups of people come to our head-quarters in Americus to be trained for work in our Habitat projects in developing countries. At one or more times during their training, I will have a session with these prospective International Partners. Many of the trainees are young people, just out of college. They have decided to serve overseas with Habitat for Humanity for three years before going on to something else in their lives. Invariably, I talk to them about "the theology of the hammer" and "the economics of Jesus." I tell these young people to build the Habitat houses in the areas where they will serve in such a way that they would be proud to go back many years later to show the houses to their grandchildren.

Our philosophy of building strong and sturdy houses was tested in August 1991, when Hurricane Bob roared through Cape Cod, Massachusetts. The first house built by Habitat for Humanity of Cape Cod, located in the Wellfleet community and occupied by Bob and Laurie Harding and their two daughters, was in its angry path. The house came through the storm without losing a shingle.

A year later, in August 1992, another truly awesome test came when Hurricane Andrew tore through south Florida, leaving utter devastation in its wake. Literally thousands of houses were flattened, and countless others were so severely damaged by the storm that they were uninhabitable. Amazingly, Habitat houses were not seriously damaged, even though some of them were right under the eye of the hurricane or close to the main path of the storm. A bold headline in the *Miami Herald* exclaimed, "Tally: Habitat 27, Andrew 0." The article under that headline related that not a single Habitat house was sufficiently damaged to cause the homeowners to move. The story was quickly picked up by other newspapers across the nation, and it was also run repeatedly on radio and television.

I flew to Miami a few days after the hurricane to see for myself what had happened. Local Habitat officials drove my party through the waste-land of south Dade County. Practically everything had been flattened, especially near the center of the storm's path.

We visited many of the Habitat houses. They literally looked as if they had been built after the hurricane! One house had the limb of a tree driven right through the roof and down into one of the bedrooms. But, that was the extent of the damage.

A house in Homestead was squarely under the eye of the storm. It was occupied by Irma Cordero and her family. Houses and other structures all around her house were lying flat on the ground or were gone! Her house, though, was only minimally damaged. Some windows were broken, a few shingles were missing, and a small porch had flown to parts unknown, but the house was intact. The family was still living in it.

I inquired about what it was like during the hurricane. Irma's son, Carlos, explained: "It was scary. We were told to evacuate because the storm would come right through this neighborhood, in full force. So, we went to a friend's house a few miles to the north."

Carlos went on to tell how the winds blew and the rain penetrated everything. He said they all thought they were going to die. Much of the house they were staying in was destroyed.

The next morning, he said they drove back to their house. The closer they got, the worse the destruction was. Carlos said his mama began to cry. "What are we going to do?" she wailed. "We have no place to live. Our house is gone!" There was no consoling her. Then, Carlos said, they arrived at their block. Turning the last corner, they could see their house still standing, with very little damage. "Mama continued to cry", he said, "but the tears changed from sad ones to tears of happiness and thanksgiving."

In the weeks following, as I traveled across the country for various speaking engagements, total strangers would approach me in airports to comment about our houses in south Florida. (They would see the Habitat for Humanity bumper sticker I have on my briefcase. These bumper stickers are important to "the theology of the hammer." I tell audiences all across the land and around the world that we have no doctrine in Habitat for Humanity since we are not a church, but merely a servant of the church. But, I go on to say, we do have one doctrinal point and that is, if you don't have a Habitat bumper sticker on your car, you are living in sin! So that I will be totally "Habitat righteous," I have a bumper sticker on our car and one on my briefcase!) Anyway, numerous people noticed my bumper sticker and said to me, "I see you are with Habitat for Humanity. God bless you. I heard that your houses didn't blow away in south Florida!"

Many people asked how I could explain the Habitat houses remaining virtually unscathed, while houses all around them were destroyed. A news reporter in Phoenix, Arizona, asked me that very question when I was there for a series of speaking engagements. I explained by telling him there were three reasons. "First," I said, "Habitat builds its houses on rocks."

"Rocks? Where did you get all those rocks in south Florida?" he queried. "I thought there was only sand in that part of the country."

"Oh no," I responded. "There are rocks if you know where to look for them."

"Well," he continued, "tell me where you found all those rocks for your houses."

"In the Bible," I replied. "Don't you know the Bible? It plainly says that you should *always* build on rocks and not on sand because houses built on sand will be destroyed in times of storms, but houses built on rocks will endure."

"Oh!" he exclaimed. "What's the second reason?"

"We put love in the mortar joints, and that love really holds the houses together."

The reporter was beginning to look incredulous. "What's the third reason?" he inquired.

"The third reason is that Habitat houses are built largely by volunteers, many of whom are not all that sure of themselves as builders. So when the rules say put two nails in a board, they put ten! Hence, a hurricane doesn't have a chance against a Habitat house."

I went on to explain that we do emphasize quality construction in Habitat. I pointed out that, since people are not working for money, their only "pay" is the satisfaction of a job well done and a sense of being about the Lord's work, which should be done right.

In practical terms, this means that volunteers do take time not only to properly nail all boards down, but also to install hurricane clips to the roof trusses and correctly nail the shingles on so that the high winds of a hurricane or other storm cannot penetrate the house and start the process of tearing it apart. (Let me emphasize that the same care about quality construction is taken whether the building is done in a rapid fire blitz-build or during slower paced construction. Some of the houses in Miami that stood during the hurricane had been blitz-built during the Jimmy Carter project in 1990.)

In Louisiana, no Habitat houses were blown down by Hurricane Andrew, either. We did not have any houses in the direct path of the storm and only a few on the periphery; however, none of them were seriously damaged.

Several years earlier, when Hurricane Hugo had ripped through South Carolina and portions of North Carolina, no Habitat houses had been torn up. Even though there were no news reports about those houses, they did indeed stand—another testament to the enduring quality of Habitat construction.

On January 17, 1994, a major earthquake hit Los Angeles. Eight Habitat houses were near the epicenter in the town of Pacoima in the San Fernando Valley. These houses, unoccupied but almost finished, were not damaged in any way by the earthquake. Additional Habitat houses in other areas of the city were, likewise, not damaged.

Of course, I am neither saying nor suggesting that Habitat houses will never be damaged by a hurricane, earthquake, or other disaster. I *am* saying that there is a correlation, although not perfect, between quality building and a good result when times of testing come. Also, there is a mystical, you-cannot-always-explain-it connection between building on those biblical rocks and applying that "love in the mortar joints" and the outcome when testing arrives—a connection that leaves me and many others in awe.

As scores of Habitat houses are being built in south Florida, south Louisiana, and on the island of Kauai in Hawaii for victims of Hurricanes Andrew and Iniki, and as we begin to help rebuild in Los Angeles, we continue to apply "the theology of a well-built house." One never knows when the next storm will blow in or earthquake hit.

"A well-built theology" is equally as important in building strong human relationships and in building up the people who live in the Habitat houses. For that reason, we have nurturing committees to work with Habitat homeowner families beginning with the date of their selection and continuing long after the houses have been finished.

Many people ask me, as I travel and speak across the country, "What happens to the people who move into the Habitat houses? What difference does a Habitat house make in the life of a family that receives one?"

I answer by reminding my questioners that love makes things grow, and Habitat is about sharing love—the love of God that causes the most growth.

I could tell so many stories, but I will share only a couple to illustrate.

In 1988, in Melbourne, Florida, the Bowsher family received the second Habitat house built by that affiliate. Beverly Bowsher, mother of the family, had learned about Habitat for Humanity in 1987 when she was stuffing old newspapers into a broken window in their decrepit trailer home. As she pushed the paper into place, in a desperate attempt to keep out the cold night air, she happened to notice an article about Habitat for Humanity. She began to read it. At the end of the article, she saw a phone number. She decided to call.

Beverly felt that, perhaps, her family would qualify for a Habitat house because of their low income and need. Her husband, Fred, was recovering steadily but slowly from emergency heart bypass surgery, a situation aggravated by his hard work of digging clams to bring in much-needed income.

Beverly made the call to South Brevard Habitat for Humanity, submitted an application, and, after a period of time, her family was chosen. For many weeks, the whole family worked alongside scores of Habitat volunteers to finish the house. Dedication day in 1988 was one of the happiest days ever in the lives of the Bowsher family.

Five years later, in January 1993, Beverly was asked to speak at the annual Carpenter's Club breakfast of South Brevard Habitat for Humanity. With much emotion, she recounted her family's story of falling into poverty and despair. She told about Fred's serious heart condition. "But," she continued, "Habitat entered our lives, and we, as a family, have been transformed."

She told how her husband's health dramatically improved and how he went back to school and got a high school diploma. Currently, she said, he is the manager of a mini-storage center in Melbourne. The children, she went on, had done well in school. Their eldest son had married, their only daughter enrolled in Brevard Community College, and the two youngest sons were in the eleventh and seventh grades. Beverly and Fred had taken in her three nieces from her hometown in Indiana after their mother died.

In closing, Beverly exclaimed, "Habitat for Humanity has not only provided us with a house. You have given us a foundation for our lives!"

Another wonderful success story is from Greensboro, North Carolina. Barbara Taylor Bray moved into her new Habitat house in October 1990. Since that time, she has been almost a blur of activity. Twice she has gone on Global Village work camps to help build Habitat houses in Honduras (the sister project for Greensboro Habitat). She has become an eloquent spokesperson for Greensboro Habitat, fulfilling engagements in churches, at civic clubs, and with other groups. Barbara also sings and has used that talent to benefit Habitat for Humanity.

When Linda and I were in Greensboro in October 1993, Beverly handed me a note that read, in part,

> Once I became a part of Habitat, my life has never been the same. In addition to the many activities you know about, I want you to know that I now have my own business. Three of us homeowners have opened a women's crafters business and *we are excited!*
>
> Thank you for giving us the opportunity to start a new life. Praise Jesus for everyone in Habitat who makes unfortunate people have a chance to begin a new life. God is a God of a *second chance!!*
>
> His Grace is sufficient,
> Barbara Taylor Bray
> President

Barbara, her husband Leroy, their daughter, Tambra, and son, Don-Taé, will make it. Barbara just needed a chance and a little love—that is what Habitat provided. Now, she is giving back and continuing to receive, too.

Across the land and around the world, local Habitat groups are constructing well-built houses and fostering the solid growth of the homeowners. This is the result of faithfully and diligently applying "a well-built theology." We take people where we find them and build them up, both in terms of solid construction and good "people building."

Biz Ostberg, long-time director of Appalachia Habitat for Humanity in Robbins, Tennessee, told of attending a "Revival '93" event in Kingsport, Tennessee, in September. In a speech about her house, one of the new homeowners said, "You looked beyond my faults and saw my need." That is what we try to do in this ministry. Once we see the need, we try to fill it as fully and completely as we can. Problems and disappointments come, but we are most encouraged with how often we get a very good result, both in terms of excellent workmanship on the Habitat houses and in positive changes in both the homeowners *and the volunteers* who work with them.

The theme of "a well-built theology" is so clearly stated in a beautiful song written about Habitat for Humanity by Norton Wade of Augusta, Georgia. (When Norton wrote this song in 1990, he was president of Augusta Habitat for Humanity.) The words for that song, "The Excitement is Building," are shown below, and the music can be found in the appendix. Note the emphasis on building both solid houses and the people who will live in them.

"The Excitement Is Building"

The Excitement Is Building, people working hand in hand
Picking up their hammers, picking up their nails, . . . and
They're building firm foundations, raising the kind of walls
That will keep a family sheltered, in a home that'll never fall.
And the excitement Is building, and it's spreading to every land
With the message of the one who died with nails in outstretched hands.
No we're not just slinging hammers, we're not just nailing nails,
'Cause we're building on the promises of a love that'll never fail.

We have the chance to build a new community
Full of hope and dreams,
A better Habitat for Humanity;
People hand in hand,
Working together to bring shelter to the world.

The excitement is not just building, the excitement is alive,
God's people helping God's people to do more than just survive.
With our partnership with each other we can ease a family's sorrow,
And with our partnership with God we can build a new tomorrow.

We have the chance to build a new community
Full of hope and dreams
A better Habitat for Humanity;
Join us and hand in hand
We'll work together to bring shelter to the world

Another musician who is helping to put up well-built Habitat houses and promote the building of better human relations is Gregory McCallum of Chapel Hill, North Carolina.

Greg (a young concert pianist, church musician, and piano teacher), received a bachelor of music degree from the University of Maryland, an artist diploma at the Hochschule School for Music in Wurzburg, Germany (where he was a Rotary Scholar), and a master of music degree from the Eastman School of Music in Rochester, New York. Always an honor student, Greg has won many prizes in piano competitions across the United States and in Germany.

In July 1992, he participated in a Habitat for Humanity Global Village work camp in Cantel, Guatemala. The experience had a profound effect on him, leading him to write movingly about working there with the local people:

> I will never forget the smiles of the little children and the proud parents in Cantel. As we worked side by side, we not only built solid homes that would withstand an earthquake, but we also built a firm foundation for hope, peace, and better international understanding.

Greg said that the experience in Guatemala not only changed his personal view of life and what is necessary to achieve happiness, but it also changed the direction of his career as a concert pianist.

Soon after returning home from Guatemala, Greg came up with a novel idea for generating needed funds for Habitat houses both in the United States and abroad. Why not use piano hammers and classical music, he thought, to raise funds for Habitat? He discussed his idea with a friend, and they came up with the slogan, "Building Houses with Music." A logo was created consisting of a piece of music torn into the shape of a house.

Greg's first concert was held in November 1992, in Chapel Hill. In 1993, three more concerts were held in various locations in North Carolina. One of the concerts raised $35,000 for Habitat's work in Orange, Durham, and Alamance counties. Greg's personal goal is to perform at least ten Habitat concerts a year throughout the country and raise many thousands of dollars for more well-built Habitat houses. His motto is, "Let the eighty-eight hammers of the piano swing into action so that other Habitat hammers can also swing into action to build, repair, or renovate an ever increasing number of Habitat houses around the world!"

Greg, incidentally, is not the only person who has been inspired by a Global Village work camp. Anne Carson of Solomons, Maryland, went to Hungary in the summer of 1993. She described her experience as "an adventure of a lifetime and a glimpse into the revolution of hope taking place in Hungary through Habitat for Humanity's concept of community rehabilitation and body-and-blood-of-Christ house building." Since returning home, she has been writing and speaking extensively about what she witnessed in Hungary. She has become a tremendous ambassador for Habitat in Hungary, raising both awareness and funds for the growing work there.

Every year, hundreds of people go out to serve in these one- to three-week work camps that include six to thirty persons each, then return to share with others what they experienced. In 1993, sixty-five Global Village work camps were organized and dispatched to Nicaragua, Papua New Guinea, the Philippines, Guatemala, Hungary, India, Tanzania, Mexico, and other countries. These work camps included people from the United States, Canada, Japan, Australia, Ireland, New Zealand, and France.

David Minich, former international partner who directs the Global Village program, expects over one hundred groups to be sent out in 1994; that number should steadily rise in following years. These Habitat partners are a vital part of helping put up more and more well-built houses and telling others about the work so that they, too, can get involved.

A final dimension of "the well-built theology" of Habitat for Humanity is that of the environment. Concern for the environment is a growing issue in just about all segments of our society. The religious community, in particular, is beginning to be sensitized on this issue. For example, Timothy Weiskel, head of Harvard University's divinity school's Seminar on Environmental Values says that, "Change is afoot, as interest in the link between ecology and theology grows among clerics, theology students, and ordinary parishioners."

New organizations that link theology with ecology are springing up such as the North American Coalition on Religion and Ecology and the North American Conference on Christianity and Ecology.

In October 1993, the Evangelical Environmental Network was launched. Evangelicals for Social Action are leading the new network in conjunction with World Vision. "The purpose of the new evangelical environmental movement" explained David McKenna (president of Asbury Theological Seminary and a key leader of the group), "is to articulate and promote a 'biblically grounded and scientifically informed' approach to today's environmental crisis." The EEN is part of a larger National Religious Partnership on the Environment. The other partners are: The National Council of Churches, the American Catholic Bishops' United States Catholic Conference, and a broadly based Jewish coalition.

More and more, in the years ahead, we will see the connection made between environmental issues and the religious community.

Habitat for Humanity has always been concerned with doing more than just "building a bunch of houses." We have had the vision from the beginning of developing viable, stable communities, as well as building individual houses that are strong and durable.

My awareness about the environment was heightened tremendously in August 1992, when I met then Senator Albert Gore. He gave me a copy of his new book, *Earth in the Balance: Ecology and the Human Spirit.* I read the book immediately and was deeply impressed both with his scholarship and with the power of his arguments concerning the enormity of the problem in regard to the environment. It was sobering reading.

As a consequence of my heightened awareness, in October 1992, I made a proposal to the Habitat for Humanity International board meeting in Minnesota that a department of the environment be created within Habitat for Humanity. The board instructed me to write a mission statement (including purposes, guidelines for implementation, and goal) for the proposed new department and to bring this statement to the midwinter board meeting in Americus in February 1993 for action. I wrote the requested statement and presented it to the board for action. With few changes, it was unanimously approved.

Habitat for Humanity is rapidly becoming the largest home builder in the United States. Within a few years, I fully expect Habitat to be the largest home builder in the world. That position puts a great responsibility on the shoulders of the leadership of Habitat for Humanity to deal boldly and positively with the whole issue of the environment. We must, as an organization and as a movement, set a good example as environmentalists.

In August 1993, my long-time friend and dedicated Habitat partner David Ewing was engaged to set up our department of the environment and start it functioning. A veteran of over thirty years as a physics professor at Georgia Southwestern College in Americus who has had an almost lifelong involvement with environmental concerns, David was very qualified for this task.

Among issues being addressed by the new department of the environment are: (1) use of recycled building materials, (2) better attic insulation to conserve energy, (3) radiant insulation barriers, (4) tree-for-tree program to replant trees that are used for lumber in Habitat houses, (5) individual and community organic gardens, (6) recycling by homeowners, (7) water conservation, (8) development or discovery of alternative building materials that are more environmentally benign, (9) information and education programs about Habitat's role in environmental protection and conservation, and (10) user-friendly environmental guides for both industrialized and non-industrialized countries.

The department of the environment wants to interface and work closely with other environmental groups, both Christian and secular— groups like Floresta located in San Diego, a Christian group doing reforestation in the Dominican Republic, and Trees for Life in Wichita, Kansas (an organization that promotes the planting of fruit trees in developing countries). ECHO in north Fort Myers, Florida, promotes gardening, especially in areas where resources are minimal. The National Wildflower Research Center in Austin, Texas, advocates landscaping for home and public areas with indigenous wildflowers. Uniquest, with offices in Salt Lake City, Utah, is an urban-waste sawmilling operation.

Green Cross, which originated in the former Union of Soviet Socialist Republics but no longer operates there, is becoming increasingly active in the United States. It encourages local groups to take responsibility for their neighborhoods and promotes environmental awareness and action.

One of the largest tasks facing the department of the environment is to work ever more closely with all Habitat for Humanity groups around the world to help them become more environmentally conscious and active. Already, a lot is going on. For example, when I visited our Habitat work in twenty-four different locations in western Uganda in May 1993, I was amazed to discover the high degree of environmental awareness. Every time we dedicated a Habitat house, one or more trees were planted. Furthermore, I saw numerous Habitat nurseries where literally hundreds of trees were being grown. In one place, Habitat leaders were talking about developing a Habitat forest!

In Lynchburg, Virginia, the local Habitat organization built an entire house out of recycled materials! In Homestead, Florida, a 200-house model ecological community is being planned.

So, the environment is a vital dimension of "a well-built theology." John Donne (seventeenth-century preacher, poet, and essayist) said, "No man is an island." In like manner, no house stands alone. No family exists in isolation. We must concern ourselves always with the "big picture." That is why "a well-built theology" includes the house, the people who built and funded it, those who live in it, and the larger community and world in which the house is located.

This multi-faceted theology that mandates doing things right at all levels and in all relationships—including those between people and God, between people and the earth, and among all of us on the earth—is moving us inexorably forward in our quest to get everybody in the world into a decent place to live. With God as our helper, guide, and strength, we are getting there!

Note

[1]See chapter 8, "The Economics of Jesus," in my book, *Love in the Mortar Joints.*

Tally: Habitat 27, Andrew 0

All S. Florida homes
by nonprofit builder
withstood hurricane

All 27 South Florida homes built by Habitat withstood hurricane

(Newspaper headlines used with permission of the Miami Herald)

A construction crew puts the finishing touches on a newly completed Habitat house in Homestead, Florida, part of rebuilding efforts after the devastation of Hurricane Andrew. (Photo by Julie Lopez)

Chapter 10

A Theology for the World

The actor Paul Newman, who is well-known for his charitable giving to causes he believes in, has long been a faithful contributor to Habitat for Humanity.

A few years ago, he sent a generous gift from his company, Newman's Own, Inc., which markets his famous salad dressing and other products. I contacted his office to ask if Mr. Newman had any preference about where the money should be used. The response was that I should make a list of proposed Habitat projects to receive the money. I made the list immediately and mailed it to him. I included several locations in the United States to receive most of the money, but I also listed some places in developing countries such as Mexico and Nicaragua.

A few days later, I received a phone call from Paul Newman. He wanted to discuss the list. "Why have you included countries outside the United States?" he inquired. "The money I gave you was made from sales in the United States. I think we should use the money in this country. But I want to hear your thinking on this matter before I make my final decision."

I thanked him for his call and for his gift. I then assured him that we would honor his designations for the money, whatever they might be. I went on to tell him, however, why we proposed designating some of his gift for the countries indicated and why Habitat for Humanity builds both in the United States and in other countries.

First of all, I said, it is good religion to have a worldwide concern and ministry. God is not an American citizen. God's love is universal and our expressions of love should be the same. We should put no artificial boundaries on our various expressions of love.

Next, I continued, as a matter of enlightened self-interest, we should help people where they are so they do not feel compelled to move to the United States. I reminded him that most people all over the world would prefer to stay where they are, if they can make a decent life for themselves and for their families in their homelands.

I went on to argue that, should we totally succeed in eliminating poverty housing and homelessness in the United States without alleviating these problems in Mexico, Honduras, Guatemala, Nicaragua, and other such countries, the pressure would build for more and more people to move to our country. While we have long had a policy of accepting "your tired, your poor . . . your huddled masses yearning to breathe free," as the Statue of Liberty proclaims, this country can absorb only so many immigrants. The answer is to help people have a good life—including a modest, but good and solid house—where they are.

Mr. Newman said that I had convinced him, and that I should leave the designations as I had them except to add a couple of new countries to the list to make sure that we were even-handed in supporting work in countries with differing political philosophies. We simply lowered the amounts designated for some of the countries in order to have some funds for the new ones.

As I said in chapter one, I have always felt that this ministry of providing decent shelter for poor families should be worldwide in scope. The work was begun in Georgia, but the next project to be launched was half a world away, in central Africa in the country of Zaire. The work then spread to Texas, Guatemala, Florida, Uganda, South Carolina, Tennessee, and eventually into all fifty states of the U.S. and to over forty other nations.

I am often asked if I am surprised at how Habitat for Humanity has grown in such an incredible way. I respond by saying that I am not surprised at the growth in the rural South of the United States and in developing countries, because that is where I saw the greatest need and also the possibility of an organization like Habitat responding to it. My biggest surprise, and really amazement, is that this ministry continues to take root and flourish in places as diverse as Los Angeles, California, and Santa Ana, El Salvador; Bombay, India, and Bonners Ferry, Idaho; Santa Cruz, Bolivia, and Pest Megye, Hungary; and Mezquital Valley, Mexico, and Port Moresby, Papua New Guinea. It just seems to work everywhere.

The universal acceptance of "the theology of the hammer" is confirmation that this whole movement is the Lord's work, and that those of us in leadership positions should forever remain in an attitude of humble awe of what God is doing through this exploding venture of faith and love in action. We should *never* try to put brakes on it or restrict it in any way. Rather, we should give free rein to the moving of the Spirit and guide the work in accordance with God's will, always seeking to expand it for the benefit of more and more people throughout the world.

This expansive and constantly expanding nature of the work, which embraces the whole world and leaves no one out, is a vital part of "the theology of the hammer." As stated elsewhere, the God who has called us to this task of eliminating poverty housing and homelessness and the same God who sustains us in the continuing challenge before us is a God of 100 sheep (Matt 18:12-14), including the prodigal son (Luke 15:11-32) and the lost coin (Luke 15:8-10). In other words, God is a God of the whole crowd. God's love extends to all, and ours should, too.

In chapter two, I quoted Henri Nouwen's reminder that the original meaning of the word "theology" was "union with God in prayer." In line with that meaning is a phrase made famous by an early monastic writer, Evagrius of Pontus (346–399): "The theologian is the person who prays; the person who prays is truly a theologian."[1]

I like that definition. I pray, therefore I am a theologian. If you pray, you, too, are a theologian. The only question is to what extent we go in praying and how much of an effort we make in trying to connect with God and to be guided by His will.

I believe in prayer and in the power of prayer. I believe that through prayer we *begin* to know God's will. Then, as we act on what we understand and continue to pray, more of God's will becomes clear to us. This process of praying and acting, then acting and praying draws us closer to the heart of God and to His perfect will for our lives and the whole world.

Based on my personal experience of prayer and acting on what I believe to be God's will, I have come to the unshakable conclusion that God's love is universal. God has no favorite race and no favorite nation. All people everywhere are the equal objects of God's love.

I do acknowledge that the Jews were God's chosen people and that through them, God revealed Himself to mankind in many special ways. However, in the fullness of time, God sent to this earth His only Son, Jesus of Nazareth, a flesh-and-blood son of the Jewish people. Through Jesus, salvation is available to all people of all nations throughout the earth.

This is my personal belief that is shared by millions of others throughout the United States and around the world. Millions more, though, do not believe as I do. Even so, I am firmly convinced that God's love extends to all—Christian and Jew, Muslim and Hindu, Buddhist and Jain, believer and infidel, totally devoted and entirely secular, friend of God and enemy of God. God's love leaves nobody out, and my love should not either. This theological understanding drives "the theology of the hammer" around the world, steadily building more and more houses in more and more countries.

Jimmy Carter has been especially helpful in encouraging support of the work of Habitat for Humanity outside the United States. As a former president, he obviously has a strong and special love for his country. He knows, however, that a great country like the United States, which has been so blessed with natural resources and with so many talented and dedicated people, has a particular responsibility to be a blessing to other people and other nations that have not been so generously endowed. (Other developed countries, too, of course, have the same responsibility.)

Since the beginning of his personal involvement with this work in 1984, he and his wife, Rosalynn, have consistently championed the work of Habitat that is being done in other lands. He has encouraged our program of tithing from U.S. affiliates and those in more developed countries. On his frequent trips around the world, he has visited Habitat projects or has made personal contact with Habitat leaders in Central and South America, Africa, Canada, and Eastern Europe.

In Nicaragua, Jimmy Carter rode for hours on rough and winding roads to visit a Habitat project in the northwestern part of the country. With the president of Nicaragua, he laid blocks and participated in the dedication of several Habitat houses. In Peru, he helicoptered to a Habitat building site high in the Andes mountains, and as has been reported elsewhere, President Carter has also led work projects in Mexico and Canada.

In 1996, the Carters are scheduled to spend a week blitz-building Habitat houses in Hungary with Kalman Lorinz, the "mad Hungarian" who does such an incredible job of leading Habitat's work in that eastern European nation.

The strong endorsement of Habitat's worldwide work by President Carter grows out of his personal conviction about the world and his belief that people of faith and prayer should act to the best of their ability to make things better for people everywhere. He has been, and continues to be, a great inspiration to me and millions of other people who are now involved in one way or another with the work of Habitat for Humanity.

For me, the year 1993 was a banner one in regard to making connections around the world with people who are either strongly interested in the ministry of Habitat for Humanity or who are already actively involved in the work. My experiences of visiting with literally thousands of people in a dozen countries reconfirmed my already strong belief in the rightness of our policy to operate globally and expand the work around the world as rapidly as possible.

My year of unprecedented travels started in January with a visit to England and Northern Ireland. Tom Jones, who heads our Habitat International office in Washington, D.C., had gone over some weeks earlier with Mark Abraham, Habitat's director of the upper Midwest region of the United States. Those two men had made arrangements for a speaking tour and a series of meetings for me with various leaders, churches, church agencies, and other groups to explore the possibility of launching the ministry of Habitat for Humanity in the United Kingdom.

For a week, Tom and I raced from one engagement to another in London, Oxford, and Banbury, England; and Belfast and Derry, Northern Ireland. Two dedicated Christian men, David Stapleton of Banbury and Ian Whitehead of London, were our primary contacts in England, while

Peter Farquharson and Peter McLaughlin of Belfast and Paddy Doherty and Pat Johnson of Derry were our primary contacts in Northern Ireland.

The result of the visit was the establishment of Habitat for Humanity offices in Banbury, with David Stapleton as director and in Belfast, with Peter Farquharson as director. I am optimistic that strong Habitat organizations will emerge in both places in the months ahead.

In mid-February, Linda and I departed on a truly amazing five-and-a-half-week journey around the world to visit Habitat work in the countries of Indonesia, New Zealand, Australia, the Philippines, and India. We also arranged to visit people in the Republic of Korea who were seeking to start Habitat's ministry and to visit our daughter, Georgia, in France on the way home. She was studying for a year at a University in Angers, southwest of Paris, and had set up a meeting where I could speak about Habitat for Humanity while we were there.

On our way to Indonesia, we stopped in Hawaii, where several activities had been planned on the island of Kauai. Rick Hathaway of our international headquarters in Americus had been dispatched to head up the effort to form a local Habitat organization to rebuild following the devastation of Hurricane Iniki.

The highlight of our time on Kauai was visiting the first Habitat house, which was nearing completion. Located on Hawaiian homelands in an area called Anahola, the house was being built for the Marti family: Sal and his wife, Agnes, and their four beautiful children—Salva, Summer, Christina, and Maja.

We drove to the house after church on Sunday to have lunch with the family and other Habitat friends and partners. The day was sunny and bright, and the building and site were absolutely spectacular. The modest, but beautiful, house was perched on a small plateau between steep, majestic mountains to the rear and a sweeping expanse of sloping mountainside to the front that descended to the bright blue Pacific Ocean.

As we shared our sack lunches on the front porch, we could occasionally see a humpback whale surface in the distance. The view and all the surounding scenery were so fantastic; it was almost unreal. I do believe that Habitat house has the most magnificent view of any Habitat house in the whole world. It was awesome!

Incidentally, in the months following our visit, the work in Kauai continued to make great progress. In September, on the anniversary of the hurricane, a big blitz-build was held: Seven houses were built in seven days. A hundred volunteers came from twenty-one states on the mainland, while many others came from three other islands of Hawaii—Oahu, Maui, and Hawaii. Over 250 volunteers from Kauai helped, also.

Many churches contributed, providing volunteers and funds from both Kauai congregations and additional ones from other Hawaiian islands and the mainland.

By the end of 1993, the new affiliate on Kauai had completed seventeen houses and had plans to build fifteen more in 1994. (Rick Hathaway left Kauai in October 1993 to help with launching Habitat in Korea, but I'm getting ahead of myself again.)

After leaving Hawaii, we headed for Pontianak (a city on the big island of Borneo in the country of Indonesia), with intermediate stops in Tokyo, Singapore, and Kuching, Malaysia. In Pontianak, we were met by Mark and Gai Case and their lovely young daughter, Daniella. Mark and Gai had been Habitat International Partners in Indonesia since December 1990, after a previous three-year stint with Habitat in the Philippines. The Cases had arranged for a Mission Aviation Fellowship (MAF) plane to fly all of us to the village of Serukam, northeast of Pontianak.

The forty-five-minute flight was very interesting. We enjoyed the beauty of the hilly countryside as we flew at low altitude. Soon, we were descending for the landing. The runway was very narrow and short. The pilot, a real expert, simply dipped down between two big hills, passed right over a barbed wire fence, and came zooming in on the bumpy landing strip.

At Serukam, we were the guests of Bethesda Hospital and Nursing School that is operated by the Conservative Baptist Mission of the United States. Also on the hospital grounds was the Bamboo River International School with a grand total of seven students—among them Daniella—in grades one to six.

Joining us the first evening, in addition to the Cases and Doctors Beth and Bert Ferrell (medical missionaries who had been serving there since the mid-1960s), were Simson and Laura, new Habitat partners working with Mark and Gai. (In that part of the country, many Indonesians use only single names.) This young couple was delightful. They were very shy, primarily due to the language barrier, but obviously gentle and kind and quite competent. Mark and Gai planned for them to take over leadership of the Habitat work in the area after their departure.

We stayed overnight at "Beth's Motel and Coffee Shop," the guest house for the mission station. It could accommodate up to twenty people, but that night the Cases and the Fullers were the extent of the guest list. The place was not exactly on the beaten tourist path! Accommodations were very spartan, but adequate. The rain on the tin roof easily lulled us to sleep.

The next morning we were up at 4:30. After eating a quick breakfast, we loaded into a van and drove for about an hour on a narrow paved road to the small town of Benkayang—where Mark, Gai, and Daniella had lived for six months when they first arrived in the region. During that time, Mark and Gai "commuted" to the small village of Sinto deep in the forest where Habitat for Humanity was making a start in Indonesia. Their first task had been to build a modest house for themselves in the village, which was completed in July 1992. It was exactly like the ones to be built for the local people. Since that time, they had finished six more houses, and an additional six were nearing completion. We were eager to see the houses and meet the people.

After visiting for a few minutes with a couple of missionary families in Benkayang, we drove several kilometers to a small settlement along the road called Peranok. Sinto was a six-kilometer walk from this village.

Our party started the trek at seven o'clock. Up and down hills we walked, crossing marshy areas and passing fields of rice and forested mountainsides. For an hour and a half we trudged along until, finally, we were at Sinto, a village of about 200 Dyaks, the dominant race of Borneo. Very handsome people with rich brown skin and coal-black hair, they made their living largely by raising rice and collecting rubber. Their traditional houses were extremely simple, constructed of sticks and mud or, sometimes, rough-hewn boards. The roofs were fashioned of whatever they could find to try to deflect the rain—a few pieces of tin, some boards, or palm branches. The place looked drab and bleak.

We were officially greeted by a host of the local people, who had fashioned a "welcoming gate" made of bamboo, palm branches, and flowers. They had also made small garlands of flowers to go around our necks.

After passing through the "gate," we continued on through the old part of the village before emerging into the new section. Scattered across the small valley and hillside were the dozen new Habitat houses. All were two-story, with an open space under one side to serve as a porch or lounging area. The houses were simple and yet attractive and quite functional for the local lifestyle.

The initial event on the agenda—for which the entire village population had assembled, as well as about 100 visitors from neighboring villages—was a number of traditional dances. Next was a whole series of speeches welcoming us to Sinto, followed by a hog-calling contest. I delivered my best rendition of a hog call, to the delight of the crowd, but a little wisp of a woman—with a wizened, wrinkled face and only a few teeth—was the clear winner. Any hog within a mile would have heard her!

At lunch time, rattan mats were spread on the ground, and everyone was served a delicious meal of salted fish, green beans, chicken, bamboo shoots, cassava leaves, rice, and tea. It was a feast by anybody's definition.

After lunch, the program continued. I spoke about the biblical foundation of Habitat for Humanity. Then, the new houses were dedicated and Bibles presented to the families receiving the first twelve houses. (An additional thirteen houses would be completed there over the next few months.)

The cost of each house was approximately $600 to be repaid over ten years. Homeowner family members were required to put in "sweat equity" in helping to build their own house and houses for their neighbors.

Next, motorcycles were provided to visit other nearby villages that would soon start building Habitat houses. Linda rode with Simson, I rode with an evangelist named Lucas, another evangelist named Jimin joined the motorcycle brigade, and Mark and Gai set out on a fourth motorcycle.

Others in our party, including the children and the driver, walked back toward the van as we roared off down a narrow path in the opposite direction. Our driver would meet us with the van later in the day at a pre-determined location for the long drive to Pontianak.

The first village we visited was Padang Pio, a distance of three or four kilometers from Sinto. After a short visit, we rode a few more kilometers to a church that had been built half a century earlier by the Regions Beyond Mission.

In the big yard in front of this country church were several hundred people. Another decorated "gate" had been built leading into the church. On top was written, "Welcome Millard and Linda Fuller." In front of the gate was a long line of leaders from the surrounding villages. Linda and I walked slowly down the line, shaking the hands of everyone. Then, we passed through the gate and went directly into the church.

The place was packed quickly. The first event was drinking coconut juice. Some men whacked off the tops of the coconuts with machetes in such a way that little holes could be poked through and straws inserted. We then sipped the raw, warm juice.

With refreshments disposed of, the program started. Various people shared greetings, after which Linda and I both were asked to speak. Mark interpreted for me and Gai for Linda. We expressed our joy over being in the country and region, and we encouraged the people in their plans to launch the work of Habitat for Humanity in their villages. We pledged our support and continuing prayers as their new venture got underway.

At our various stops in four villages after we left Sinto, Mark explained the work about to begin. Under the supervision of Simson, ten Habitat houses would be built in each village, for a total of forty more houses. Half of the house payments from Sinto would go into this new phase to show how the payments would help people in other locations as well as in their immediate area.

Late in the afternoon we rode the motorcycles to the rendezvous point with the van and piled in for the four-hour ride to Pontianak. In the late night hours, we pulled into the driveway of the home of David and Janet Bonney, Canadian missionaries of the Conservative Baptist Church.

Arrangements had been made for us to stay overnight with the Bonneys before leaving the next morning for Jakarta. Close to midnight, we crawled into bed, thoroughly exhausted but full of excitement about what we had experienced and also full of anticipation about the next phase of our journey.

Mark and Gai accompanied us to the capital city because they had arranged a full agenda of activities for us there. On Sunday, we raced from church to church practically all day long. In the morning, I spoke at a charismatic worship service at the Hilton Hotel and at the regular Sunday morning services at the Jakarta Community Church and Kebayoran Baptist Church. In the evening, I spoke at All Saints Anglican Church. All of these services were in English, and most of the members or visitors were Americans—except in the Anglican service where many people were from England, Canada, Australia, and New Zealand. Most of the services were packed. In fact, at the Baptist church not all of the people could get a seat; many sat outside and looked through the open rear doors of the church. That congregation, too, was the most diverse, with many Indonesians in attendance.

Lively interest in Habitat for Humanity was evident at all services, especially in the blossoming work in Indonesia. Several people said they wanted to contribute financially, and the Baptist church expressed interest in organizing a work group to go to the villages we had visited and help build the Habitat houses. (Later in the year such a group did go to help for a week.)

On Monday and Tuesday, we negotiated the incredible traffic of Jakarta as we visited with church and church agency leaders. We also continued to talk with Mark and Gai about the future of Habitat for Humanity in Indonesia. Their vision is to have Habitat work underway in all of the twenty-seven provinces of the country by the end of the decade. They wanted to continue their work in the villages for about six more months and then move to Flores, a province in the eastern part of the country, where a lot of interest had been expressed in Habitat for Humanity.

In the years ahead, Mark and Gai want to move from province to province, starting new projects and then leaving trained local leaders to continue running them. They would like to have at least two more teams of International Partners to join them in this proliferation effort.

Already, they had in hand proposals for Habitat projects from more than a dozen provinces including Flores, where the Cases moved in late 1993 to launch the ministry of Habitat for Humanity in that province.

Mark and Gai are totally committed to the work of Habitat for Humanity in Indonesia. They feel a strong call from God to work there. We are fortunate to have these dedicated servants of Christ on the Habitat team in that country.

On March 2, Linda and I flew out of Jakarta on our way to New Zealand. We were met at the airport in Auckland by Ian Hay and his wife, Diana.

Ian had first learned about Habitat for Humanity a few months earlier from *Builder* magazine, the official publication of the U.S. National Association of Home Builders. He had then been in touch with me by both phone and letter, and he had also talked by phone with some people in Kansas City, Missouri, about Habitat. Then, Peter Vanderburg, executive director of Habitat for Humanity in Australia, visited Ian and others in Auckland who had developed an interest in the ministry. Two of those other people who had a keen interest in Habitat for Humanity were Michael Powell and Carl Graham, two Aucklanders who had worked with Habitat in the United States.

When Ian had decided to come to the United States in November 1992 for a builders conference, he had also made the decision to visit the international headquarters in Americus. On Sunday, we went together to Maranatha Baptist Church in Plains for Sunday School and the morning worship service. Ian was able to talk to Jimmy Carter about his dream of bringing Habitat for Humanity to New Zealand. President Carter encouraged him greatly, as did many other Habitat folks.

Ian was the right man for this job. He was president of the Keith Hay Group, the second largest home building company in New Zealand, and a committed Christian, with a strong desire to make his life count for the betterment of the less fortunate people of the world. When Ian found out that Linda and I planned to be in Australia in early March, he said his group would organize quickly to build the first house and have it ready for us to dedicate if we could come over for that event. I told him to go to work, and that we would squeeze in at least a day on our already tight itinerary—which we did.

After a busy morning meeting with New Zealand's Habitat board members, conducting interviews and meeting with church leaders, we drove south of Auckland (about fifty kilometers) to the small town of Pukekohe, where the first Habitat house in New Zealand was to be dedicated. Ian told us it had been built in just twenty-six days. The newly formed group that had built the house was Habitat for Humanity of Franklin. The family to receive it was a young Maori couple, Charles and Moana Herewini and their three year-old son, Josiah, who had been living in a decrepit "caravan" (a small camper-like vehicle).

When we arrived at the site, we found a beautiful rectangular house with a bright blue roof. It was completely finished except for a little wallpaper that had not yet been put up. A large, attractive sign out front proclaimed that this was a Habitat for Humanity house and acknowledged the various suppliers who had contributed materials for it.

A crowd of over 150 people gathered for the dedication, in spite of very overcast and rainy weather. The local mayor and his wife were present along with the traditional leader of the Maori people. After several speeches, a choir of Maoris sang a couple of traditional songs. I was then invited to address the crowd. I first taught them to yell "Oyée!"—the cheer of affirmation from Zaire. I then told them about "the theology of the hammer," including the requirement of putting Habitat bumper stickers on their cars to avoid "living in sin." At the conclusion of my talk, I presented a Bible and a house key to Charles and Moana. The Herewinis were invited to respond. Charles, the spokesman for the family, was very emotional and made his talk with great difficulty. His words of appreciation and tears touched everyone very deeply. He stood there content to get soaking wet from the rain because, in the Maori culture, it is considered a blessing.

Afterwards, everyone was invited to tour the house. The invitation was extended in a dramatic fashion by Moana's mother, who stood at the front door and yelled in a loud voice in her native tongue. Linda and I were beckoned to enter the house first. As we approached the door, the woman took me by the arm and pulled me down toward her face. For a moment, I thought she was going to kiss me right in the mouth! But she just wanted to rub noses with me, a traditional greeting and sign of love and respect in her culture. In the several minutes following, both Linda and I rubbed noses with all of the Herewini family members and several other people. It was fun!

Later in the afternoon, I was interviewed for the television evening news program for the nation. In the evening, I spoke at a large dinner attended by business, government, church, and community leaders of Auckland.

The next morning, Linda and I boarded a plane headed for Sydney, Australia. We felt good about our time in New Zealand and about prospects for Habitat's future there. In the months following, incidentally, the work did continue to progress. By the end of 1993, one more house had been built by Habitat for Humanity of Franklin. Habitat for Humanity Christchurch was officially recognized in October 1993, and plans were well underway to launch a Habitat organization in Wellington.

In Sydney we were met by Peter Vanderburg. He, Vera Randall (Habitat International board member), and Gordon Moyes (president of the Australia Habitat board) had planned a busy weekend agenda for us.

The afternoon was filled with interviews with various media people. That evening, we attended a formal dinner with many top government, civic, and industry leaders at the Intercontinental Hotel.

The next day we attended a conference in Castle Hill, a suburb of Sydney, for representatives of the nine Habitat affiliates in Australia and for people from prospective Habitat groups in three other cities. Both Linda and I addressed the Habitat leaders. In the afternoon, the whole group toured the Blacktown Habitat project where five townhouses were being built.

On Sunday, I spoke at the two morning services at the Hills Christian Church in Castle Hill, where Vera Randall and some other Habitat leaders are members.

On Monday, Linda and I were winging our way to Manila, the Philippines, to be met by Gloria Ison, national director of Habitat for Humanity in that island nation; Sam Bandela, area director for Habitat for Asia and the Pacific; and Norma Caluscusan, one of the founders of Habitat for Humanity in Dumaguete City and a member of the Habitat International board.

We had a truly incredible week in the Philippines, including three busy days in Dumaguete City, located in Negros Oriental Province in the southern part of the country. The highlight of our time in Dumaguete City was our visit to the two big Habitat projects, Balugo and Candau-ay. These projects are located on opposite sides of the city garbage dump. Many of the new Habitat homeowners moved directly from the garbage dump into their new Habitat houses in one or the other of these new communities.

We toured Balugo first, where eighty-eight Habitat houses had been completed. A huge crowd waited at the entrance to the community. A sign over the main street welcomed us.

As we and scores of happy mamas and papas and their equally happy children walked through the clean streets—with neat Habitat houses on both sides, surrounded by a great profusion of flowers and lush vegetable gardens in several places—I realized that we were probably seeing the best Habitat project in the world. It was absolutely like walking through a story book.

At one house, a woman handed me a note. When I read it, I wept.

> Welcome to our family, who has now risen from being a squatter member of so many long years. And God give us shelter through your help. We thank you so much.
>
>   Mr. and Mrs. Felix Leonora Fidila

Norma informed us that the people were faithfully making their house payments that were being used to build more houses in Candau-ay. Undoubtedly, by any standards, Balugo was the best Habitat project I had seen anywhere in the world. That special community is a great inspiration to me.

After touring Balugo, we walked through the garbage dump where, unfortunately, quite a few people still lived.

On the other side in Candau-ay, sixty Habitat houses had been completed, and twenty-five more were under construction. The houses in Candau-ay were of the same high quality as in Balugo; another great Habitat community is in the making. A work camp from Japan was busy in Candau-ay, and another work group was scheduled for the following week.

In the afternoon, we participated in an official dedication of ten newly completed houses in Candau-ay. Several people spoke at the dedication, including Linda and me and the mayor of Dumaguete City, Agustin Perdices. As a grand conclusion, the mayor told the excited audience that the city would keep on donating land to Habitat so that the work could continue without interruption in the effort to rid the city of slum housing and provide everyone with a good house. The mayor said he was pledging the additional land as an encouragement not only to the local Habitat organization in Dumaguete City, but to affirm a challenge I had issued the previous day in a meeting with Habitat representatives from Dumaguete City, General Santos City, and Midsayap. The latter two cities are on the island of Mindinao.

My challenge was to spread the work of Habitat for Humanity to at least half of the seventy-five provinces in the Philippines and initiate the building of 10,000 houses by the end of the decade. At that time, Habitat for Humanity had organizations in six locations in four provinces—the three locations named above plus Manila and two groups in northern Luzon, in Saguday and Balintocatoc.

The mayor went on to say that he wanted to personally pledge one house a year—a commitment that would be 30,000 pesos or about $1,000 —plus his own labor to help build! A tremendous cheer went up from the crowd. (The mayor was a man of his word, too. The next day, at City Hall, he presented me with his personal check for the first 30,000 pesos. His action inspired others. Within a few days, I learned later, several other individuals and organizations made similar pledges.)

After the mayor spoke, the new homeowners were asked to share with the audience. Some completed their talks just fine, but many wept. Apparently, in their culture it is considered shameful to cry in public, so the homeowners would desperately try to restrain their tears. To keep from crying, they would laugh—with the result that often they were crying and laughing at the same time!

Following the talks, we went to each of the ten houses and dedicated them. Then, we came back to the central area of the community and presented each family with a Bible and keys to their new house.

It was a joyous day!

On Thursday afternoon, Linda, Sam Bandela, and I flew back to Manila. Gloria Ison had a packed agenda for us that included visits to the three Habitat projects being run by Metro Manila Habitat for Humanity; a visit to "Smokey Mountain," the huge garbage dump in Manila where 3,000 families make their living scavenging in the refuse; a dedication service for the new national office for Habitat; a reception and dinner with some key national leaders; preaching at two Sunday morning services at Union Church of Manila; and dedicating the 500th house in the Philippines.

The three Habitat projects in metro Manila are Topsville, Rotaryville, and SNKI (an acronym for Samahang Nagkakaisa Sa Kamarin, Inc.— generally known as Kamarin).

In Topsville, Habitat is building 146 houses. At the time of our visit, thirty had been completed. Each house was only twenty-four square meters, but the very poor families who received them feel they are palaces; they are, compared to the miserable hovels they moved from in the squatter settlements.

The Rotaryville project is on the east side of Manila in an area called Mandaluyong. 192 Habitat houses are planned on two and a half hectares (about six acres) of land. The project is sponsored by the Rotary Club of Mandaluyong and the Rotary Family Helper Project in cooperation with the Christian Children's Fund. On the site, we buried a "time capsule" to mark the beginning of the work.

Kamarin, the oldest project in Manila, is located on the outskirts of the city in a place called Kalookan City. Mark and Gai Case worked there before moving to Indonesia. At the time of our visit, 118 houses had been built at that location, and thirty-two more were planned. Philippine Christian University provided the land. On a very hot Sunday afternoon, we gathered at Kamarin to celebrate five years of work by Habitat for Humanity in metro Manila and to dedicate the 500th house built in the country. That house was occupied by a widow, Maria Aranas, and her three children.

Representatives from the two Habitat projects in northern Luzon, including Ken Bristol (the International Partner there), came to Manila to meet with Linda and me. Jeff and Loraine Janes from Mindinao also came. As I had done in Dumaguete City, I challenged all Habitat people in the

Philippines to work to establish Habitat in at least half of the provinces and to build 10,000 houses by the year 2000.

Later in the year, Karen Foreman, director of the Habitat affiliates world-wide department of Habitat for Humanity International, had a meeting with leaders of all Habitat projects in the Philippines; the challenge was officially accepted as a goal for the country. I believe they will accomplish it! While the need for decent housing is enormous in the Philippines, the good news is that we can build Habitat houses there for only $900 each. What a difference that small amount makes in the life of a family.

On Monday morning, March 15, we boarded United Airlines flight 808 for Seoul, Korea, flying not only to a different country, but also into winter!

At the Seoul airport, we were met by Dr. Wong-In Koh, Mr. Jin Myung Choo, and Mrs. Soon Ja Kim. No Habitat organization existed in Korea, but these dedicated Christians and many others had learned about the ministry and wanted to bring the work to their nation.

In numerous meetings, we discussed how to form a national Habitat for Humanity organization that would recognize and approve local affiliates throughout the country.

We became acquainted with Dr. Keun-Mo Chung, who had been named president of the forming Habitat organization. A very distinguished and well-known man in Korea, he is ambassador for nuclear energy cooperation for the South Korean government. He is also a dedicated Christian layman for whom faith is central to his life.

I spoke at a public meeting at the Christian Union Center and appeared on a national T.V. program with Dr. Chung. We also toured some areas with low-income housing in Seoul.

When we departed two days later for India, Linda and I felt good about our time in Korea and left convinced that Habitat for Humanity would eventually get started in that country.

Our plane arrived in Bombay at midnight. We were met by a couple of the leaders of Bombay Habitat for Humanity, who drove us immediately to a nearby hotel for two hours' sleep before coming back to the airport to catch a plane to Cochin in Kerala State in southern India. From there, we drove to Koovapally, a three-hour ride further south.

The highlight of our stay in Koovapally was a gigantic parade and celebration marking the completion of 360 Habitat houses. The exciting events began with a motorcade to the center of the city. Then, we left the cars, walked down a street toward the site for the celebration, and were met by literally thousands of people.

A big sign over the street welcomed Linda and me to the city. As we approached the sign, huge numbers of firecrackers were set off. We continued to walk down the middle of the street, with people lined along both sides waving and cupping their hands in front of themselves in the traditional Indian greeting. A dozen young men were dancing and banging on some musical sticks in front of us as we made our way on toward the place of the meeting.

Babu and George Thomas, two of the key Habitat leaders, had told us that almost all of the people from the 360 Habitat houses would be present for the parade and celebration. They were, and they brought all their friends and neighbors, too!

As we arrived at the podium for the celebration, another huge round of firecrackers exploded. We took our seats, and the program began. There were many speeches and special songs. Then, keys to the most recently built house were presented, and the happy homeowner gave a rousing speech of appreciation. Linda and I were asked to speak and so was Faye Inlow, our International Partner in Koovapally. The program concluded with the national anthem of India.

The next day, we dedicated several more Habitat houses. Then we were off to Bangalore where we spent two days visiting and dedicating half a dozen houses, including the 100th house built by that affiliate. I was also privileged to preach in two churches on Sunday morning.

Something wonderful happened at that 100th-house dedication. It was held in a community on the outskirts of Bangalore called Jakksandra. We were escorted there by Mr. Augustine, director of Bangalore Habitat for Humanity, and Father Aloysius, president of the board of directors of the affiliate.

At the edge of the community we were met by several hundred people. Traditional fragrant garlands were placed around our necks. We were then led by a band to the house, which had been very colorfully decorated for the occasion.

After the ceremony—which included cutting a ribbon that was draped across the front door, presenting a Bible to the new homeowners, and entering the house for some refreshments—a community meeting was held in the street in front of the house.

A tarpaulin had been spread over the area. Several groups sang and danced. I was asked to speak. I talked about how Habitat for Humanity is a partnership—with God, the homeowners, the local Habitat organization, and the people in India and the United States and other places that contribute to the work. I pointed out that anyone can be a partner in the ministry. All that is needed is a loving heart and a desire to share and be a part.

When the program ended, our party started walking toward our vehicle, parked about 100 yards away. As we entered the crowd, all of a sudden, a little girl appeared in front of me with her hand outstretched.

At first I thought she was begging, but then I saw the coins in her hand. No more than eight or nine years old, she wore a simple dress—a village girl, but with a radiance that immediately made me feel that I was looking into the face of an angel.

I was startled for a moment until I realized that she wanted to give the money to me. She wanted to be a Habitat partner! I lifted her into my arms and announced to the crowd what she was doing. A great cheer went up. "Father Aloysius," I said, "this little girl has given these rupees to me. I now want to give them to you to use in buying more materials to build more houses for needy families." Another cheer went up.

I put my new little partner down, and our party continued to walk toward the car. The band struck up a lively tune. Hundreds of children were all around us with as many as possible holding our hands. I was so happy that I started jumping and dancing. Others joined in, laughing, dancing and jumping. We continued like that all the way to the vehicle. Even after we got in, the people, especially the children, did not want us to leave. It was a very special, unforgettable experience.

The next day, I spoke at Hudson Memorial Church, the largest Protestant church in Bangalore. It is a congregation of the Church of South India. The pastor, Rev. A. P. Ranjan, told me that the church has about 700 families or over 3,000 members. In that service, I was introduced to a new custom I had never seen before: All participants leading the service had to remove their shoes. The church could not hold all of the people who came, so at least 100 people stood outside. Loudspeakers had been installed to broadcast the service to those persons.

After that service, we rushed to St. Anthony's Friary Catholic Church. After I challenged the congregation, as I had done at the Hudson Memorial Church, to get involved with the work of Habitat in Bangalore, a couple of businessmen came forward to offer their assistance.

On Monday morning we were off to Hyderabad, our last stop in India. When we emerged from the baggage claim area, we were absolutely swarmed by Habitat people. They had come from our projects in Rewari (south of Delhi), Bonghir, Guntur, Hubli, Bombay, Khammam and, of course, from Twincities Habitat for Humanity in Hyderabad and Secunderabad.

These people had fragrant garlands for Linda and me and Sam Bandela, who was still traveling with us. By the time all of them were placed around our necks, we could barely see. Each of us must have been wearing at least fifteen garlands weighing thirty pounds!

When we walked outside we were greeted by huge banners that welcomed us to the Twincities. After posing for pictures, we went by caravan, with horns blaring, to downtown Hyderabad.

The first event was a big public service at the Centenary Baptist Church. With representatives present from most of Habitat's ten affiliates in India, I challenged them to set a goal to establish Habitat in all twenty-five states of India and build at least 20,000 houses by the end of the decade.

In Secunderabad, we dedicated the 1,000th Habitat house in India. It had been built for a man named Kristo Dass and his wife, Susehla, and their three children—Nathaniel, Merline, and Steven. Kristo Dass means "servant of God," and Susehla means "woman of good and strong character."

Following another big rally at the Centenary Baptist Church that evening, we were ready to leave India. We had had a fantastic time in the country. I felt the people would work diligently to meet the challenge of 20,000 houses by the year 2000. They will need some continuing help, but they are determined and hard working. Habitat houses in India cost an average of only $1,000, and each house provides good and decent shelter for five to a dozen people.

By the end of 1993, a total of 1,175 houses had been built in India, and we were at work trying to establish one or more Habitat organizations in the area hit by the devastating earthquake in September of that year, as well as in several other locations.

At last, we flew from India to France to spend a few days with our daughter, Georgia, before returning home. In addition to our personal time with her, we met with the people of a house church in Angers that Georgia had been attending; it was a joy to tell them about the work of Habitat around the world.

On Saturday afternoon, March 27, Linda and I arrived in Atlanta and drove directly to Americus, thus ending a long and tiring, but very rewarding journey.

We had only a week to get ready for the big 20/20,000 project. Immediately thereafter, we were off to San Diego, California, for the Habitat West regional meeting, with a brief trip into Mexico to visit the site of the 1990 Jimmy Carter Work Project and tour new sites where additional building had been started.

In May, I went to east Africa to visit our work in Uganda and to attend the Habitat International board meeting, which was to be held in Entebbe. (Linda did not accompany me on that trip.)

My experiences in western Uganda had a profound effect on me. I had worked and traveled in Africa for years, but what I saw and learned in my travels this time opened my eyes to new possibilities for not only Uganda, but for all of Africa and the world.

Our work in Uganda was inaugurated in the northern town of Gulu in 1980. Over the next few years, we built nearly thirty houses there.

Unfortunately, the project had to be discontinued due to political turmoil and violence.

In 1987, work was reopened in Uganda, in the far western part of the country, in the town of Kasese. From there, over the next six years, Habitat projects spread to three other areas—Masindi, Rwenzori, and Semliki. Building was initiated in a total of twenty-four locations, and nearly 600 houses had been constructed.

Ray and Gloria Cunningham, career missionaries with the Lutheran Church in Tanzania, went to Uganda to work with Habitat for Humanity in 1988, after a one-year stint with Habitat in Tanzania. Their career with Habitat followed twenty-seven years with the Lutheran Church.

Ray and Gloria, as Habitat project developers with the mandate to proliferate the work throughout the country, not only helped build a great number of houses in Kasese, but they also organized a week-long work-study project that brought eighty people from all over Uganda to Kasese in June 1992 to learn how to start Habitat for Humanity in their home towns and villages.

With the good help of Bishop Zebedee Masereka and other church and community leaders in Kasese and other International Partners, the pioneering work-study project in Kasese was a huge success. The people worked in the mornings each day. In the afternoon they heard lectures and were able to ask questions about the philosophy of Habitat—how it worked, how to apply for a local project, and so forth. As a result, the people returned home fired up and determined to bring Habitat for Humanity to their communities. Within a few months, Ray and Gloria had received 110 proposals for new Habitat projects!

That presented a problem because the existing procedure for initiating a new Habitat sponsored project was to present the proposal to staff in Americus, arrange a site visit, and—if that staff person approved—then submit the proposal to the international program committee of the board (which met three times a year), and—if the committee approved— recommend the new project to the full Habitat International board.

If the board approved the project, two things happened simultaneously. First, the new project was accepted as an official Habitat for Humanity project. Second, funding for the first phase (usually 100-200 houses) was approved. Still, construction could not begin until an International Partner was located, trained, and sent to guide the new project.

Ray and Gloria realized that it would take years for this procedure to run its course with the large number of proposals they had. In the meantime, the enthusiasm and momentum would be lost. They argued that a faster approval system should be adopted to give these local groups authority to proceed, even before funding from the U.S. could be provided. Ray, especially, was forceful in his arguments, and he was increasingly convincing as we traveled together and saw first-hand what was actually happening in the work in western Uganda.

I was part of a small group of board members consisting of Maggie Chrisman and her husband Bill from Phoenix, Arizona; Norma Caluscusan from the Philippines; and Kathryn Kinnamon from Lexington, Kentucky. While we toured with Ray and Gloria, other board members were visiting Habitat's work in Kenya, Tanzania, and Malawi.

For four days we traveled throughout western Uganda, visiting places like Bundibugyo, Lake Katwe, Munkunyu, Ntandi, Katunguru, and Kisolholho. Everywhere we went, huge crowds greeted us.

In Kisolholho, a village on the border of Zaire, over 6,000 people attended a big Habitat rally. Toward the end of a long program, I was called forward and told they were making me a king of the Bakonjo (the local tribe). I was presented with a long spear and a shield, symbols of kingly authority. In response, I said I appreciated their gesture of kindness and affirmation, but that I did not wish to be a king. My desire, I said, was to follow as faithfully as I could, the King of kings, the Lord Jesus. I continued by telling the large assemblage that the presentation reminded me of a king in the Bible, David. On occasion, when he was very happy—too happy for words or song—he would dance to express his joy. I said that I was so full of joy and happiness because of the love of the people toward me and our whole group and because of the wonderful Habitat work we had seen, that I—like King David—could not adequately express how I felt with mere words or song. So, I said, I would dance for them. I then took the spear in one hand and the shield in the other and danced for several minutes in the middle of the big circle of people. They hollered and clapped and laughed to their heart's delight.

Houses were being built in great numbers everywhere we went, and the people were raising a lot of the money for the building. At every rally, auctions were held. Sheep, goats, chickens, art objects, paintings, food items, cloth, and other things were sold to the highest bidder with the money going to Habitat. Donations of money were dropped into a big box, along with written pledges for future support. I had never seen anything like it!

The Habitat houses in Uganda cost about $500 to $700. It occurred to me that, with enthusiasm and determination, people in Uganda could probably raise those sums, even though they are extremely poor, just as Habitat volunteers in the United States raise $35,000 for a Habitat house, or volunteers in Canada, New Zealand, or Australia raise $50,000 for their modest Habitat houses. Everything is relative, and, if we give a financial boost from time to time, it is amazing what can be accomplished.

As I pondered deeply about the matter, I realized that we, as an organization, had inadvertently stifled the growth of the work in developing countries. Our cumbersome and lengthy approval process, linked totally to funding and personnel, delayed the expansion in countries like Uganda.

In the United States and other developed countries, our approval procedure was to encourage formation of local groups. As soon as the groups had raised a specified amount of money (in the U.S., $3,000), had a board of directors, were incorporated, and signed the Habitat Covenant, they were approved and recognized as official Habitat for Humanity affiliates. They could then raise more money and build, renovate, and repair houses. Habitat International—through regional offices in the United States and national offices in places like Canada, Australia, and New Zealand—could monitor the work of local groups; give advice; and provide resources such as manuals, training sessions, regional meetings with workshops, seminars, and general meetings—all designed to equip the local people and keep them motivated as they steadily expand their building efforts to achieve the goal of eliminating poverty housing in their respective areas.

The consequence of our differing procedures for developed and developing countries was that growth in countries like the United States was phenomenal, while growth in countries like Uganda was much slower. The irony of the whole situation was that the *greater need* is in places like Uganda!

I went to the board meeting in Entebbe convinced that we must change our procedure. I felt that we must liberate the people from the existing cumbersome approval process. To my delight, the board enthusiastically accepted this idea. Warren Sawyer, head of the international program committee, wrote a resolution that was unanimously passed by the board. It became known as the Entebbe Initiative. The essence of the resolution was to form national Habitat for Humanity organizations in all countries where we have Habitat work and to empower them "to encourage the formulation, timely approval, and operation of new Habitat projects in all countries." The resolution concluded, "Henceforth, all projects around the world will be simply known as Habitat projects."

The resolution instructed staff to develop a national covenant to be approved at the board meeting that was to be held in Waterloo, Ontario, Canada. Such a covenant was developed, and it became official by action of the board in October 1993. (See a full copy of the Covenant in the appendix.)

One change was made at the follow-up board meeting, and that was to refer to all local Habitat for Humanity organizations as *affiliates*, instead of two distinct groups previously termed "affiliated projects" (in so-called developed countries) and "sponsored projects" (in developing nations). Also, the national covenant provides for the *expectation* of tithing by all affiliates to work in other countries. This means that even Habitat affiliates in developing countries are expected to tithe to affiliates in still other developing countries. In this way, we promote everybody helping everybody! That is not bad theology, and it certainly is good psychology and development strategy.

The new procedure allows newly forming groups to apply to their national organization for affiliation with Habitat for Humanity. As soon as they are organized, have a board of directors, and sign the covenant, they can be approved and are authorized to raise money and begin building Habitat houses. (Habitat International will confirm or ratify the newly approved affiliates from time to time.)

After approval, any Habitat affiliate anywhere in the world is free to apply to Habitat for Humanity International for funding; we will approve such requests as resources allow us to do so. Funding will be granted on the basis of need and in accordance with the biblical principle of "feeding strength." In other words, we will reward diligence and effective local work in raising money and good stewardship in building methods, techniques, and so forth, adding more money where there is legitimate need for additional money and where local funds are being wisely used. This philosophy is deeply rooted in the parable of the talents, where the good steward is rewarded and given more while the slothful steward who "buries his talent in the backyard" has even that talent taken from him (Matt 25:14-30).

I believe this change is a watershed happening in the evolving movement of Habitat for Humanity. I fully expect to see explosions of growth all over the world as we have already been seeing in the United States for the past several years.

As an example of what is to come, consider the following written by Ray Cunningham in the October–November 1993 Uganda Habitat newsletter concerning a new affiliate in eastern Uganda called Elgon Habitat for Humanity:

> We were awakened by the singing of the volunteers who had already started gathering. It was Wednesday morning. With Mr. Mboneraho, our new National Coordinator for Uganda, and Mr. Sam Mutongole and Mr. David Gudo, field educators, we proceeded to the building site.
>
> Our group immediately joined in by helping bring the sand in plastic bags, old cooking pans, an old wooden wheelbarrow and a still older metal wheelbarrow that had to be pulled with a banana fiber rope to get it past the muddy spots. Others brought bags of lime to mix with the sand to make mortar.

The many volunteers had no building tools. They were trying to lay bricks using their hands as trowels! With no basins for carrying the mortar, they were using old cooking pans. In the afternoon, I went to get some trowels, a spirit level, plum bob, two spades, and three metal basins. My return with these items was met with great enthusiasm!

Other than for these tools, all their expenses were paid with money the people had raised. We were told that one man had given a cow, another a goat, a lady had contributed 10,000 shillings ($10), and quite a bit of money had been raised from auctioning off many donated items.

On Thursday, the work went faster. Little children passed bricks along a long line to the site. Primary school students gave up their lunch break to help pass bricks.

By Friday afternoon, the work had reached wall-plate level. On Saturday, the rafters and iron sheets were laid and nailed down and gables finished. In just four days, the house was ready! A second house was finished in five days.

I returned home from Uganda full of hope and joy because of all that happened.

In July, I took my last trip outside the United States in 1993. I went with Linda and our two youngest daughters, Faith and Georgia, and Jimmy and Rosalynn Carter to participate in the blitz-building in Winnipeg and Kitchener.[2] I have written elsewhere about this work in Canada, so I will not repeat the story here.

My extensive travels in 1993—coupled with other trips in previous years to the Caribbean, Central and South America, and other places—have fortified my belief in the correctness of Habitat for Humanity's policy of working on a worldwide basis, which is consistent with my understanding of God's word. "For God so loved the world, that He gave . . ." If God loved and gave to the world, so should I. So should you.

Thus, "the theology of the hammer" is for the whole world: starting right where you live and going out to the ends of the earth; putting faith and love to work; always doing a good job in keeping with "a well-built theology"; constantly seeking to enable people from all walks of life to participate in the mission; and forever focusing on the vision God has given us of ending poverty housing and homelessness and building both houses and the people who will live in them.

So, keep praying and hammering. "The theology of the hammer" is a movement on the move—in your home area and all around the world!

Notes

[1]*Thomas Merton: Spiritual Master, The Essential Writings*, edited and introduced by Lawrence S. Cunningham (New York: Paulist Press) 30.

[2]See chapter 5, page 60.

Millard and Linda Fuller and Habitat Asia/Pacific area director Sam Bandela join a joyous group at the dedication of the 100th Habitat house in Bangalore, India.

A happy family reaches out to touch a Bible presented during house dedication ceremonies in Uganda, Africa

Appendix

Mission, Purposes, Goal, and Guidelines
of Habitat for Humanity International, Inc.

Mission

Habitat for Humanity works in partnership with God and people everywhere, from all walks of life, to develop communities with God's people in need by building and renovating houses so that there are decent houses in decent communities in which people can live and grow into all that God intended.

Purposes

The official purposes of Habitat for Humanity are to sponsor specific projects in habitat development globally, by constructing modest but adequate housing, and to associate with other organizations functioning with purposes consistent with those of Habitat, as stated in the Articles of Incorporation, to witness to the gospel of Jesus Christ throughout the world:

(1) By working in cooperation with God's people in need to create a better habitat in which to live and work;

(2) By working in cooperation with other agencies and groups which have a kindred purpose;

(3) By exemplifying the gospel of Jesus Christ through loving acts and the spoken and written word;

(4) By enabling an expanding number of persons from all walks of life to participate in this ministry.

Goal

The ultimate goal of Habitat for Humanity is to eliminate poverty housing and homelessness from the face of the earth by constructing and building adequate and basic housing. Furthermore, all of our words and actions are for the ultimate purpose of putting shelter on the hearts and minds of people in such a powerful way that poverty housing and homelessness become socially, politically, and religiously unacceptable.

Guidelines for Implementing Habitat's Purposes

(1) Believing that the work of Habitat for Humanity is inspired by the Holy Spirit, we understand that the purposes express the hope that others may be grasped and led in yet unforeseen ministries by the Holy Spirit.

(2) Adequate housing as used in the purposes means housing and much more, and includes the total environment (e.g., economic development, compassionate relationships, health, energy development, etc.). To effect positive changes in the total environment, Habitat works in cooperation with other agencies which have expertise in specific areas.

(3) The term "in cooperation" as used in Habitat's stated purposes should be defined in terms of partnership:

(a) Partnership implies the right of all parties to engage in vigorous negotiation and the development of mutually agreed-upon goals and procedures. The negotiation in partnership should occur with each project and will include such items as defining what adequate housing means in that particular project, who are God's needy, and what local entity will control the project.

(b) Partnership further implies that all project personnel—local people or expatriate volunteers—have a primary and equal relationship in regard to all matters relating to that particular project. International Partners have an additional fiduciary responsibility to the Board.

(4) Habitat's position is one of responding to expressed needs of a people in a given area who are seeking a partner relationship with Habitat for Humanity. A primary concern in all matters is respect for persons, including their culture, visions, and dignity.

(5) All Habitat projects must establish a Fund for Humanity, and financing of houses and other ventures must be given on a no-interest basis. Each Fund for Humanity wll be funded through voluntary gifts (in cash and in kind), grants, and interest-free loans, from individuals, churches, other groups, and foundations. All repayments from houses for other Habitat-financed ventures will also be returned to the local Fund for Humanity. Finally, Habitat projects may operate enterprises which will generate funds for the local Fund for Humanity.

National Covenant
Habitat for Humanity of (Country)
and Habitat for Humanity International, Inc.

Preamble

Habitat for Humanity works toward implementing the Gospel of Jesus Christ throughout the world by working in partnership with individuals, churches and other groups, including local, regional and national Habitat for Humanity organizations. Based upon the fundamental principles set forth in God's Word, Habitat for Humanity builds and renovates houses and develops communities in partnership with low-income people and finances the houses at no profit and with no interest.

The official mission of Habitat for Humanity is to work in partnership with God and people everywhere, from all walks of life, to develop communities with God's people in need by building and renovating houses so that there are decent houses in decent communities in which people can live and grow into all that God intended.

The official purposes of Habitat for Humanity are to establish specific projects in human habitat development, by constructing simple, decent and affordable housing, and to associate with other organizations functioning with purposes consistent with those of Habitat in witnessing to the Gospel of Jesus Christ throughout the world:

(1) By working in cooperation with God's people in need to create a better habitat in which to live and work.

(2) By working in cooperation with other agencies and groups which have a kindred purpose.

(3) By exemplifying the gospel of Jesus Christ through loving acts and the spoken and written word.

(4) By enabling an expanding number of persons from all walks of life to participate in this ministry.

Habitat for Humanity's goal is to eliminate poverty housing and homelessness from the face of the earth. Furthermore, all of our words and actions are for the ultimate purpose of putting shelter on the hearts and minds of people in such a powerful way that poverty housing and homelessness become morally, socially, politically, and religiously unacceptable.

Initials by Representatives: HFHI_____ HFH of Country;_____

Article 1—Habitat Principles

The covenant guides the implementation and operation of Habitat's principles in (Country) through the cultivation and nurture of various Habitat affiliates in (Country).

(1) Grassroots Partnership: Habitat for Humanity responds to the expressed needs of local people who desire to establish a partner relationship with Habitat for Humanity. This partnership is enhanced and furthered by "the theology of the hammer" which brings people from all faiths and backgrounds together to build and renovate houses in (Country) and throughout the world.

Habitat for Humanity is based upon respect for persons and their culture, vision, and dignity. Preferential treatment or bribes are not consistent with Habitat's grassroots partnership or its stewardship ministry.

The leadership of Habitat for Humanity should be balanced and reflect the broad diversity of the population in (Country) by including people from all spectrums of life without regard to race, religious beliefs, national origin, gender, or political affiliation, so long as there is agreement with the official mission and purposes of Habitat for Humanity. Habitat for Humanity International may designate one person to serve as its representative to the National Organization's board of directors.

(2) Homeowner Participation: Habitat for Humanity selects homeowner families according to criteria which account for the demonstrated needs of a family for adequate housing, the family's financial condition and ability to repay the loan, and the willingness of the family to partner by contributing "sweat equity," i. e. participation in building of houses. When Habitat projects select homeowner families, there should be no discrimination on the basis of race, religious beliefs, national origin, gender, or political affiliation.

(3) Stewardship Ministry: Habitat for Humanity is a ministry which uses the "economics of Jesus" by seeking the blessing of God in using available resources to build houses with those in need. Habitat for Humanity appeals to the stewardship of Christians and others of good will to share and donate their resources (including time, talent, and financial resources) with the economically poor.

Habitat for Humanity's stewardship ministry transcends national borders. Habitat for Humanity International expects Habitat affiliates to support the work of Habitat for Humanity in other countries by contributing prayer and other resources. It is expected that 10% of all funds raised within (Country) will be donated for Habitat work in another country. Habitat for Humanity

International shall assume responsibility for coordinating the managing of contributed resources which are to be used in other countries.

While working in partnership with government, Habitat for Humanity International has adopted a policy which defines the use of government support and resources by Habitat affiliates. It is agreed that Habitat for Humanity of (Country) will faithfully abide by the government funds policy of Habitat International.

(4) Fund for Humanity: All Habitat affiliates must establish a revolving Fund for Humanity which is funded by gifts, grants, and interest free loans from individuals, churches, organizations and other groups. The Fund for Humanity is dedicated to constructing more Habitat houses.

House payments from each Habitat homeowner should be returned to the revolving Fund for Humanity, allowing the homeowner to help other needy people build still more houses.

The Fund for Humanity operates through the sale of houses for no profit and the financing of the house sale at no interest.

(5) Simple, Decent, and Affordable Houses: All Habitat for Humanity houses shall be simple, decent, and affordable.

Initial by Representatives: HFHI:_____HFH of Country_____

Article 2—Understandings

Specific understandings between Habitat for Humanity International and Habitat for Humanity of (Country):

(1) Habitat for Humanity of (Country) has submitted an application for status as a Habitat for Humanity National Organization; and Habitat for Humanity International has accepted the application. The parties recognize and agree that the application is included by this reference and made a part of this convenant.

(2) Habitat for Humanity of (Country) and Habitat for Humanity International are lawfully organized in their countries of residence and citizenship. The organizational and operational documents contain the provisions necessary to be a Habitat national organization.

(3) We recognize that Habitat for Humanity International and Habitat for Humanity of (Country) have entered into this covenant without assuming the other's financial and other obligations which may exist now or in the future.

(4) We recognize that the name "Habitat for Humanity" is the property of Habitat for Humanity International and has been granted to Habitat for Humanity of (Country) for use in accordance with the provisions of this covenant and can be revoked by Habitat for Humanity International in the event of dissolution of this covenant or the compromising of the integrity of the Covenant on the Habitat for Humanity program.

(5) While we do not anticipate conflict or misunderstanding, Habitat for Humanity International and Habitat for Humanity of (Country) recognize that the human condition can lead to misunderstanding and conflict. We recognize that there may need to be an opportunity for the parties to be heard in a non-confrontational setting which mediates satisfactorily the misunderstanding. We agree, therefore, to seek guidance from the Holy Spirit and Biblical Scriptures in developing an appropriate forum for such mediation, should it be needed.

(6) Habitat for Humanity International is a global ministry with many affiliates. In order to accomplish Habitat for Humanity's mission of making people aware of housing and inadequate shelter, Habitat for Humanity International presents periodic reports of Habitat's work, In providing these public reports, Habitat for Humanity International uses information provided by local Habitat affiliates and national Habitat organizations.

(7) Habitat for Humanity International and Habitat for Humanity of (Country) assume the mutual responsibility for ensuring the integrity of the

Habitat for Humanity program through a national program review and evaluation process.

Initials by Representatives: HFHI:_____ HFH of Country:_____

Article 3—Covenant Agreement

We understand and accept the responsibilities of Habitat for Humanity's ministry and, by this covenant, we commit ourselves to be stewards of this ministry by faithfully serving Jesus Christ in the mutual fulfillment of the mission, purposes, and goal of Habitat for Humanity.

Habitat for Humanity International recognizes Habitat for Humanity of (Country) as its duly constituted partner in (Country) to assist in developing Habitat affiliates in (Country) which subscribe to and implement the mission, goal, and purposes of Habitat for Humanity.

Habitat for Humanity International, Inc.

By:_____

Habitat for Humanity of (Country)

By:_____

Initials by Representatives: HFHI:_____ HFH of Country:_____

The Excitement Is Building

by Norton M. Wade

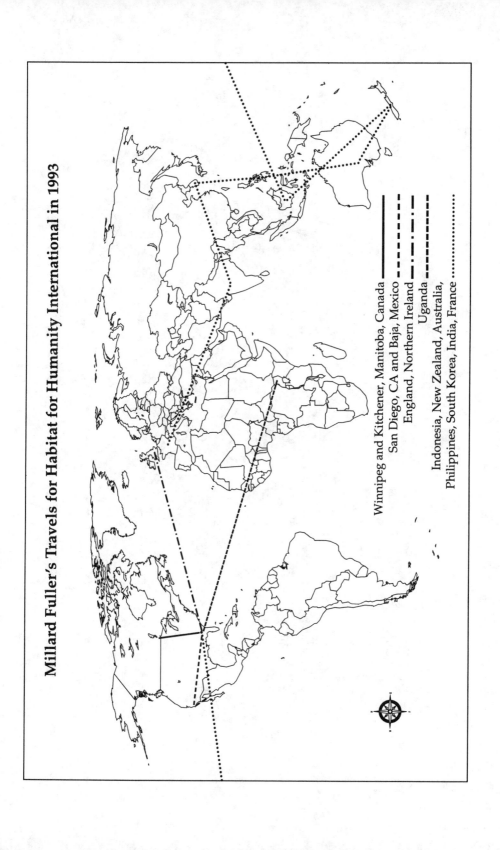

Millard Fuller's Travels for Habitat for Humanity International in 1993

Winnipeg and Kitchener, Manitoba, Canada
San Diego, CA and Baja, Mexico
England, Northern Ireland
Uganda
Indonesia, New Zealand, Australia,
Philippines, South Korea, India, France

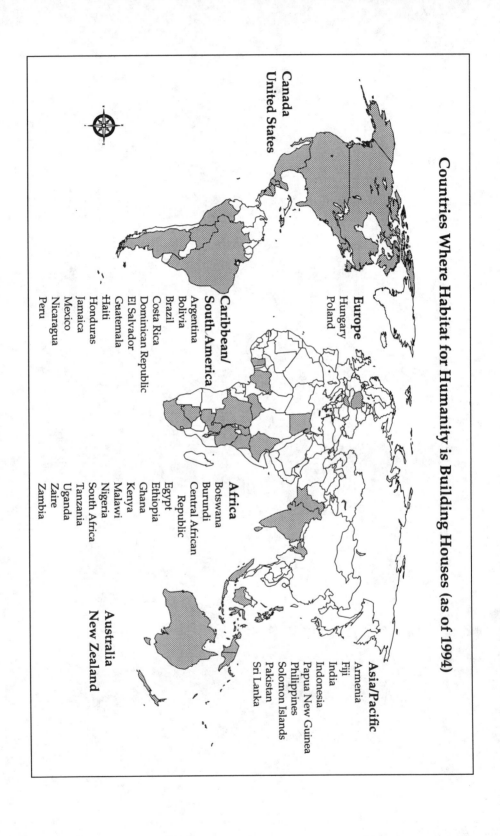

Countries Where Habitat for Humanity is Building Houses (as of 1994)

Canada
United States

Europe
Hungary
Poland

Caribbean/
South America
Argentina
Bolivia
Brazil
Costa Rica
Dominican Republic
El Salvador
Guatemala
Haiti
Honduras
Jamaica
Mexico
Nicaragua
Peru

Africa
Botswana
Burundi
Central African
     Republic
Egypt
Ethiopia
Ghana
Kenya
Malawi
Nigeria
South Africa
Tanzania
Uganda
Zaire
Zambia

Asia/Pacific
Armenia
Fiji
India
Indonesia
Papua New Guinea
Philippines
Solomon Islands
Pakistan
Sri Lanka

Australia
New Zealand